DR. ACKERMAN'S BOOK OF THE
GERMAN SHEPHERD

LOWELL ACKERMAN DVM

BB-102

Overleaf: German Shepherds photographed by Karen Taylor.

The author has exerted every effort to ensure that medical information mentioned in this book is in accord with current recommendations and practice at the time of publication. However, in view of the ongoing advances in veterinary medicine, the reader is urged to consult with his veterinarian regarding individual health issues.

Photography by: Dr. Lowell Ackerman, Dr. Zoe Backman, Christine Filler, Isabelle Francais, Jeff Greene, Judy Iby, Robert Pearcy, and Karen Taylor.

The presentation of pet products in this book is strictly for instructive purposes only; it does not constitute an endorsement by the author, publisher, owners of dogs portrayed, or any other contributors.

© 1996 by LOWELL ACKERMAN DVM

Distributed in the UNITED STATES to the Pet Trade by T.F.H. Publications, Inc., One T.F.H. Plaza, Neptune City, NJ 07753; distributed in the UNITED STATES to the Bookstore and Library Trade by National Book Network, Inc. 4720 Boston Way, Lanham MD 20706; in CANADA to the Pet Trade by H & L Pet Supplies Inc., 27 Kingston Crescent, Kitchener, Ontario N2B 2T6; Rolf C. Hagen Inc., 3225 Sartelon St. Laurent-Montreal Quebec H4R 1E8; in CANADA to the Book Trade by Vanwell Publishing Ltd., 1 Northrup Crescent, St. Catharines, Ontario L2M 6P5 ; in ENGLAND by T.F.H. Publications, PO Box 15, Waterlooville PO7 6BQ; in AUSTRALIA AND THE SOUTH PACIFIC by T.F.H. (Australia), Pty. Ltd., Box 149, Brookvale 2100 N.S.W., Australia; in NEW ZEALAND by Brooklands Aquarium Ltd. 5 McGiven Drive, New Plymouth, RD1 New Zealand; in Japan by T.F.H. Publications, Japan—Jiro Tsuda, 10-12-3 Ohjidai, Sakura, Chiba 285, Japan; in SOUTH AFRICA by Lopis (Pty) Ltd., P.O. Box 39127, Booysens, 2016, Johannesburg, South Africa. Published by T.F.H. Publications, Inc.

MANUFACTURED IN THE
UNITED STATES OF AMERICA
BY T.F.H. PUBLICATIONS, INC.

CONTENTS

DEDICATION

To my wonderful wife Susan and my three adorable children, Nadia, Rebecca, and David.

PREFACE

Keeping your German Shepherd Dog healthy is the most important job that you, as an owner, can do. Whereas there are many books available that deal with breed qualities, conformation, and show characteristics, this may be the only book available dedicated entirely to the preventative health care of the German Shepherd Dog. This information has been compiled from a variety of sources and assembled here to provide you with the most up-to-date advice available.

This book will take you through the important stages of selecting your pet, screening it for inherited medical and behavioral problems, meeting its nutritional needs, and seeing that it receives optimal medical care.

So, enjoy the book and use the information to keep your German Shepherd Dog the healthiest it can be for a long, full, and rich life.

Lowell Ackerman DVM

BIOGRAPHY

D r. Lowell Ackerman is a world-renowned veterinary clinician, author, lecturer, and radio personality. He is a Diplomate of the American College of Veterinary Dermatology and is a consultant in the fields of dermatology, nutrition, and genetics. Dr. Ackerman is the author of 34 books and over 150 book chapters and articles. He also hosts a national radio show on pet health care and moderates a site on the World Wide Web dedicated to pet health care issues (**http://www.familyinternet.com/pet/pet-vet.htm**).

BREED HISTORY

**THE GENESIS OF THE
MODERN GERMAN SHEPHERD**

Although many people intuitively feel that the German Shep herd Dog is closely related to the wolf and therefore descended from a long lineage, the truth is that the  breed is less than a hundred years old. All across Europe, shepherd dogs were used for herding livestock, and in 1889, Max Emil Friedrich

Facing page:
The German
Shepherd Dog
has achieved a
high level of
popularity
around the
world.

von Stephanitz crusaded to standardize the German Shepherd Dog (Deutsche Schäferhunde) into the breed it is today. The original standard was based on mental stability and utility, with appearance only secondary in importance. The first German Shepherd Dog was named Hektor Linksrhein, but von Stephanitz bought him and renamed him Horand von Grafrath, the first registered German Shepherd Dog, S.Z. 1 and the foundation of the breed.

The breed prospered with the efforts of von Stephanitz, and he almost single-handedly built the German Shepherd Dog Club (Verein für Deutsche Schäferhunde) into the largest club devoted to a single breed in the entire world. In 1904 the first German Shepherd Dog was brought to America, and the breed quickly gained popularity

Derived from working sheepdogs, German Shepherds have natural herding instincts that are still evident today.

The inquisitive and alert expression of the German Shepherd is easy to see in these three young pups.

(until World War I when anything German became anathema in America). During those years, the Germans made good use of these dogs as "war dogs" and "police dogs."

The reputation of these working dogs reinvigorated the American marketplace, and soon, everyone wanted a dog like Rin-Tin-Tin or Strongheart. Unfortunately, most of the dogs that were bred to fill the public's demand had a myriad of medical and behavioral problems which, once again, contributed

to the temporary downfall of the breed. Of course, during World War II, anti-German sentiment was again high, and the term "Alsatian" was preferred by American breed enthusiasts. Although the term Alsatian is still sometimes used, the term German Shepherd Dog (dog is part of the name) is the most commonly used. The German Shepherd Dog continues to be extremely popular and has been among the top five registered breeds for many years.

MIND & BODY

**PHYSICAL AND BEHAVIORAL TRAITS
OF THE GERMAN SHEPHERD**

The German Shepherd symbolizes the great protector, the perfect family dog, and the all-around community dog. A quality German Shepherd ranks among the most beautiful, intelligent, and kind of all animals. The Shepherd is de-

fined by his vitality and nobility; he is direct and fearless, confident and out-

Facing page: The classic family dog and guardian, the German Shepherd displays a love and devotion for his owners that cannot be matched.

10

going. The breed is poised and alert, well fitting his many roles as man's helper and best friend.

CONFORMATION AND PHYSICAL CHARACTERISTICS

This is not a book about show dogs, so information here will not deal with the conformation of champions and how to select one. The purpose of this chapter is to provide basic information about the stature of the German Shepherd Dog and qualities of its physical nature.

Clearly, beauty is in the eye of the beholder. Since standards come and standards go, measuring your dog against some imaginary yardstick does little for you or your dog. Just because a dog isn't a show champion doesn't mean that he or she is any less of a family member, and just because a dog is a champion doesn't mean that he or she is not a genetic time bomb waiting to go off.

When breeders and those interested in showing German

The German Shepherd Dog is a show dog of grace and style. The number one show dog of all time is indeed a German Shepherd Dog: Champion Altana's Mystique owned by Jane A. Firestone.

As herding dogs, German Shepherds were originally bred to be medium-sized dogs; however, their proficiency as guard dogs required them to become progressively larger.

Shepherd Dogs are selecting dogs, they are looking for those qualities that match the breed "standard." This standard, however, is of an imaginary German Shepherd Dog and changes from time to time and from country to country. Thus, the conformation and physical characteristics that pet owners should concentrate on are somewhat different and much more practical.

German Shepherd Dogs were originally bred to be medium-sized dogs (they were used to herd livestock), but as they were used for more and more guard work, they were bred to become progressively larger. Most adult males are 24—26 inches at the withers and bitches are about two inches smaller. The normal weight range for the breed is 66—88 pounds (30—40 kg), but a better target is about 70 pounds for females and 75 pounds for males. Adult height is typically reached by 10—18 months of age, but dogs will continue to "fill out" until they are about three years of age. Larger dogs are not necessarily better dogs. German Shepherd Dogs were never intended to be considered "giants," and the increased size might promote some medical problems that tend to be more common in larger dogs. There is some preliminary evidence that the larger members of the breed might be more susceptible to orthopedic disorders such as elbow dysplasia and hip dysplasia.

German Shepherd Dog puppies have floppy ears that may stand as early as eight to ten weeks of age or not until six to seven months of age. Some dogs have ears that never stand, which is referred to by breeders as "soft ear." Taping can correct the problem in most cases, but these animals are poor breeding choices for those interested in promoting the breed standard. Most breeders advise that you do not pet your puppy's ears backwards until they stand for fear of damaging the cartilage. However, floppy or straight, ear carriage has no health consequences. Don't look for surgical options. Being a true German Shepherd Dog has to do with genetics, not surgery.

COAT COLOR, CARE, AND CONDITION

The German Shepherd Dog comes in a variety of colors, which may be confusing to those who only associate the breed with black and tan coloring with "saddleback" markings. In fact,

German Shepherd Dogs can be black and tan, black and red, black and cream, all black, all white, sable (with various colorations), black and silver, liver, and blue. Breeders consider the white, liver, and blue German Shepherd Dogs to have conformation faults.

In the German Shepherd Dog, color is controlled by a series of genes that vary in dominance. These include the agouti, black, white, dilution, and mask series that are responsible (in combination) for the different colors mentioned. The agouti series controls the basic body color. Black body color is recessive to sable and black/tan. The black series controls pigment formation such that *BB* controls black pigmentation of the nose, eyerims, and pads, and the recessive forms *(bb)* are liver color; carriers are *Bb*. Most German Shepherd Dogs carry the dominant black series *(BB)*. White is recessive to all other colors, and both parents must carry the gene to produce white pups. The dilution series controls the "tint" of the coat color. Most German Shepherd Dogs carry dominant genes *(DD)*. Those that carry both recessive genes *(dd)* will have a blue tint. Two blues bred will produce blue pups. Carriers *(Dd)* won't be diluted but can

Although neither the American Kennel Club or The Kennel Club of Great Britain allow for a white German Shepherd Dog, many enthusiastic breeders specifically breed for this color and show them in rare breed events.

produce blue pups if mated to a blue *(dd)* or a carrier *(Dd)*. The mask series controls the color of the facial mask where E produces no mask, E^m produces a black mask, *e* is clear tan, and e^{br} produces brindle. Researchers believe that white German Shepherd Dogs carry the double-recessive white gene *(ww)* and that the color is not due to the more common white spotting gene (s^w). It should now be obvious that color combination in the German Shepherd Dog is a fairly complex science. The color of a German Shepherd Dog has no impact on its health, its ability to work, or its capacity to be a loving family member.

Most German Shepherd Dogs have a double coat of medium length and short hair on the face and limbs. Length of fur is determined by yet another gene, so dogs may be medium-coated, long-coated, or carriers of the long-coated gene. The outer "guard" hairs are shed all year long, and the woolly undercoat

The German Shepherd Dog varies in color, and strong, rich colors are most desirable. However, the color of your German Shepherd Dog has no bearing whatsoever on its health. Here are examples of a solid black and a black and tan saddle.

is "blown" twice a year, usually in the spring and fall. Some long-coated varieties actually have very little undercoat. Grooming is not difficult, but regular brushing is necessary to remove dead undercoat that accumulates next to the skin. You may think your German Shepherd Dog sheds a lot, but you'll be amazed how much fur you recover from regular brushing.

German Shepherd Dogs are fairly low maintenance, when it comes to grooming. All they typically require is regular brushing, especially when they are in the process of "blowing" their coats. When they get dirty, a hypoallergenic cleansing shampoo is preferred. A mild degreasing shampoo (e.g., selenium disulfide) is recommended for those with a tendency toward oily skin.

BEHAVIOR AND PERSONALITY OF THE ACTIVE GERMAN SHEPHERD

Behavior and personality are two qualities that are hard to standardize within a breed. In years past the German Shepherd Dog has had a bad reputation as being vicious, most of it having to do with indiscriminate breeding practices in the 1950s. At that time, the German Shepherd Dog was the most popular breed in the United States, and breeders with questionable reputations were producing a glut of pups without concern for temperament or health (hip dysplasia in the breed also reached epidemic proportions).

Although generalizations are difficult to make, most German Shepherd Dogs are alert, people-oriented, and anxious to work. This is not the breed to be tied in the backyard to serve as a watchdog. This versatile herding dog is most content when it has a job to do, and this is why so many have received recognition as police dogs, drug enforcement agents, search/rescue dogs, and guide dogs. Whether they are shy or vicious has something to do with their genetics but is also determined by the socialization and training they receive.

Behavior and personality are incredibly important in dogs, and there seem to be quite evident extremes in the German Shepherd Dog. The ideal German Shepherd Dog is neither aggressive nor fearful, but rather a loving family member with good self-esteem and acceptance of position in the family "pack." Because the German Shepherd Dog is a powerful dog and can cause much damage, it is worth spending time, when selecting a pup, paying attention to any evidence of personality problems. It is also imperative that *all* German Shepherd Dogs be obedience trained. Like any dog, they have the potential to be vicious without appropriate training; consider obedience class mandatory for your sake and that of your dog.

Although many German Shepherd Dogs are happy to sleep the day away in bed or on a sofa, most enjoy having a purpose in their day, making them excellent work dogs. They enjoy long daily walks and runs and appreciate events that involve family members. Do not let German Shepherd Dog pups run unrestricted because it can increase their risk of developing orthopedic disorders. All German Shepherd Dogs should attend obedience classes and need to learn limits to unacceptable behaviors. A well-loved and well-controlled German Shepherd Dog is certain to be a valued family member. The loyal and loving German Shepherd Dog will be your personal guard dog if properly trained; aggressiveness and viciousness do not fit into the equation.

For pet owners, there are several activities to which your German Shepherd Dog is well-suited. They not only make great walking and jogging partners but are also excellent community volunteers. For German Shepherd Dog enthusiasts who want to get into more competitive aspects of the dog world, consider these activities: obedience, showing, hunting, guarding, tracking, herding, carting, backpacking, and Schutzhund.

Although not recommended for amateurs, Schutzhund is a fast-growing competitive sport to test dogs for correct temperament and working ability.

SELECTING

**WHAT YOU NEED TO KNOW TO FIND
THE BEST GERMAN SHEPHERD PUPPY**

Owning the perfect German Shepherd Dog rarely happens by accident. On the other hand, owning a "genetic dud" is almost always  the result of an impulsive purchase and failure to do even basic research. Buying this book is a major step in understanding the situation and making intelligent choices.

Facing page: Selecting a German Shepherd puppy is not an easy process. The adorable little faces steal your heart and make it difficult to choose just one!

SOURCES

Recently, a large survey was done to determine whether there were more problems seen in animals adopted from pet stores, breeders, private owners, or animal shelters. Somewhat surprisingly, there didn't appear to be any major difference in total number of problems seen from these sources. What was different were the kinds of problems seen in each source. Thus, you can't rely on any one source because there are no standards by which judgments can be made. Most veterinarians will recommend that you select a "good breeder," but there is no way to identify such an individual. A breeder of champion show dogs may also be a breeder of genetic defects.

The best approach is to select a pup from a source that regularly performs genetic screening and has documentation to prove it. If you are intending to be a pet owner, don't worry about whether your pup is show quality. A mark here or there that might disqualify the pup as a show winner has absolutely no impact on its ability to be a loving and healthy pet. Also, the vast majority of dogs will be neutered and not used for breeding anyway. Concentrate on the things that are important.

MEDICAL SCREENING

Whether you are dealing with a breeder, a breed rescue group, a shelter, or a pet store, your approach should be the same. You want to identify a German Shepherd Dog that you can live with and screen it for medical and behavioral problems before you make it a permanent family member. If the source you select has not done the important testing needed, make sure they will offer you a health/temperament guarantee before you remove the dog from the premises to have the work done yourself. If this is not acceptable, or they are offering an exchange-only policy, keep moving; this isn't the right place for you to get a dog.

Pedigree analysis is best left to true enthusiasts, but there are some things that you can do even as a novice. Inbreeding is to be discouraged so check out your four or five generation pedigree and look for names that appear repeatedly. Most breeders linebreed, which is acceptable, so you may see the same *prefix* many times but not the same actual dog or bitch. Reputable breeders will usually not allow inbreeding at least three generations back in the puppy's pedigree. Also ask the breeder to provide registration numbers on all ancestors in the pedigree for which testing was done through OFA (Orthopedic Foundation for Animals) and CERF (Canine Eye Registratin Foundation). If there are a lot of gaps, the breeder has some explaining to do.

As soon as you purchase a German Shepherd Dog, pup or adult, go to your veterinarian for a thorough evaluation and testing. The screening procedure is easier if you select an older dog. Animals can be registered for hips and elbows as young as two years of age by the Orthopedic Foundation for Animals (OFA) and by one year of age by Genetic Disease Control (GDC). This is your dog's insurance against hip dysplasia and elbow dysplasia later in life. German Shepherd Dogs now have a relatively low incidence of these orthopedic problems because of the efforts of conscientious breeders who have been doing the appropriate testing. A verbal testimonial that they've never heard of the condition in their lines is not adequate and probably means they really don't know if they have a problem— move along.

Evaluation is somewhat more complicated in the German Shepherd Dog puppy. The PennHip™ procedure can determine risk for developing hip dysplasia in pups as young as 16 weeks of age. For pups younger than that, you should request copies of OFA or GDC registration for both parents. If the parents haven't both been registered, their hip and elbow status should be considered unknown and questionable.

All German Shepherd Dogs, regardless of age, should be screened for evidence of von Willebrand's disease, although the disease is not as prevalent in this breed as it is in some others. This can be accomplished with a simple blood test. The incidence is getting high enough that routine testing is warranted, yet the problem is uncommon enough that it should be possible to completely eradicate it from the breed.

For animals older than one year of age, your veterinarian will also want to take a blood sample to check for thyroid function and liver disease in addition to von Willebrand's disease. All are common in the German Shepherd Dog. A heartworm test, urinalysis, and evaluation of feces for internal parasites is also recommended. If there are any patches of hair loss, a skin scraping should be taken to determine if the dog has evidence of demodectic mange.

Your veterinarian should also

perform a very thorough ophthalmologic (eye) examination. The most common eye problems in German Shepherd Dogs are cataracts, persistent pupillary membranes, and retinal dysplasia. It is best to acquire a pup whose parents have both been screened for heritable eye diseases and certified "clear" by organizations such as CERF. If this has been the case, an examination by your veterinarian is probably sufficient, and referral to an ophthalmologist is only necessary if recommended by your veterinarian.

BEHAVIORAL SCREENING

Medical screening is important, but don't forget temperament. More dogs are killed each year for behavioral reasons than for all medical problems combined. Temperament testing is a valuable, although not infallible, tool in the screening process. The reason that temperament is so important is that many dogs are eventually destroyed because they exhibit undesirable behaviors. Although not all behaviors are evident in young pups (e.g., aggression often takes many months to manifest itself), detecting anxious and fearful pups (and avoiding them) can be very important in the selection process. Traits most identifiable in

the young pup include: fear, excitability, low pain threshold, extreme submission, and noise sensitivity.

Pups can be evaluated for temperament as early as seven to eight weeks of age. Some behaviorists, breeders, and trainers recommend objective testing where scores are given in several different categories. Others are more casual about the process, since it is only a crude indicator anyway. In general, the evaluation takes place in three stages by someone the pup has not been exposed to. The testing is not done within 72 hours of vaccination or surgery. First, the pup is observed and handled to determine its sociability. Puppies with obvious undesirable traits such as shyness, overactivity, or uncontrollable biting may turn out to be unsuitable. Second, the desired pup is separated from the others and then observed for how it responds when played with and called. Third, the pup should be stimulated in various ways and its responses noted. Suitable activities include lying the pup on its side, grooming it, clipping its nails, gently grasping it around the muzzle, and testing its reactions to noise. In a study conducted at the Psychology Department of Colorado State University, they also found that heart rate was a good indicator in this third stage of evaluation. Actually, they noted the resting heart rate, stimulated the pup with a loud noise, and measured how long it took the heart rate to

assessed in the PAT include: social attraction to people, following, restraint, social dominance, elevation (lifting off ground by evaluator), retrieving, touch sensitivity, sound sensitivity, prey/chase drive, stability, and en-

Puppy aptitude tests effectively show the personality of each puppy, revealing which type home and owner best suits each dog.

recover to resting level. Most pups recovered within 36 seconds. Dogs that took considerably longer were more likely to be anxious.

Puppy aptitude tests (PAT) can be given in which a numerical score is given for 11 different traits, with a **1** representing the most assertive or aggressive expression of a trait and a **6** representing disinterest, independence, or inaction. The traits

ergy level. Although the tests do not absolutely predict behaviors, they do tend to do well at predicting puppies at behavioral extremes.

ORGANIZATIONS YOU SHOULD KNOW ABOUT

The Orthopedic Foundation for Animals (OFA) is a nonprofit organization established in 1966 to collect and disseminate information concerning orthopedic diseases of animals and to establish control programs to lower the incidence of orthopedic diseases in animals. A registry is maintained for both hip dysplasia and elbow dysplasia. The ultimate purpose of OFA certification is to provide information to dog owners to assist in the selection of good breeding animals; therefore, attempts to get a dysplastic dog certified will only hurt the breed by perpetuation of the disease. For more information contact your veterinarian or the Orthopedic Foundation for Animals, 2300 Nifong Blvd., Columbia, MO 65201.

The Institute for Genetic Disease Control in Animals (GDC) is a nonprofit organization founded in 1990 and maintains an open registry for orthopedic problems, but does not compete with OFA. In an open registry like GDC, owners, breeders, veterinarians, and scientists can trace the genetic history of any particular dog once that dog and close relatives have been registered. At the present time, the GDC operates open registries for hip dysplasia, elbow dysplasia, and osteochondrosis. The GDC

Veterinary clinics provide routine examinations as well as screening services for breeding potential animals.

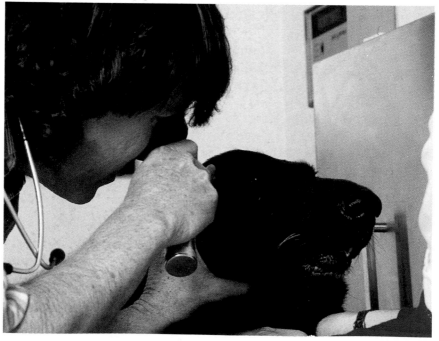

is currently developing guidelines for registries of Legg-Calve-Perthes disease, craniomandibular osteopathy, and medial patellar luxation. For more information, contact the Institute for Genetic Disease Control in Animals, P.O. Box 222, Davis, CA 95617.

The Canine Eye Registration Foundation (CERF) is an international organization devoted to eliminating hereditary eye diseases from purebred dogs. This organization is similar to OFA that helps eliminate diseases like hip dysplasia. CERF is a nonprofit organization that screens and certifies purebreds as free of heritable eye diseases. Dogs are evaluated by veterinary eye specialists, and findings are then submitted to CERF for documentation. The goal is to identify purebreds without heritable eye problems so they can be used for breeding. Dogs being considered for breeding programs should be screened and certified by CERF on an annual basis, since not all problems are evident in puppies. For more information on CERF, write to CERF, SCC-A, Purdue University, West Lafayette, IN 47907.

Project TEACH™ (Training and Education in Animal Care and Health) is a voluntary accreditation process for those in-

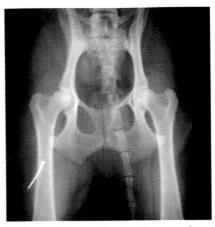

This radiograph displays a dog that received an OFA "excellent" when x-rayed for hip dysplasia. Both of his hip joints are clear of dysplasia.

dividuals selling animals to the public. It is administered by Pet Health Initiative, Inc. (PHI) and provides instruction on genetic screening as well as many other aspects of proper pet care. TEACH™-accredited sources screen animals for a variety of medical, behavioral, and infectious diseases *before* they are sold. Project TEACH™ supports the efforts of registries such as OFA, GDC, and CERF and recommends that all animals sold be registered with the appropriate agencies. For more information on Project TEACH™, send a self-addressed stamped envelope to Pet Health Initiative, P.O. Box 12093, Scottsdale, AZ 85267-2093.

FEEDING & NUTRITION

**WHAT YOU MUST CONSIDER EVERY DAY TO FEED
YOUR GERMAN SHEPHERD THROUGH HIS LIFETIME**

Nutrition is one of the most important aspects of raising a healthy German Shepherd Dog, and yet it is often the source of much controversy between breeders, veterinarians, pet owners, and dog food manufacturers. However, most of these arguments have more to do with marketing

Facing page: Your German Shepherd puppy will require a diet much different from an adult's. Be sure to check with the seller and stick to the same type of food that the puppy has been used to so as not to upset its digestive system.

than with science. Let's first take a look at dog foods, and then determine the needs of our dog. This chapter will concentrate on feeding the pet German Shepherd Dog rather than breeding or working dogs.

COMMERCIAL DOG FOODS

Most dog foods are sold based on marketing (i.e., how to make a product appealing to owners while meeting the needs of dogs). Some foods are marketed on the basis of their protein content, others based on a "special" ingredient, and still others are sold because they don't contain certain ingredients (e.g., preservatives, soy). We want a dog food that specifically meets our dog's needs, is economical, and causes few, if any, problems. Most foods come in dry, semi-moist, and canned forms. Some can now be purchased frozen. The "dry" foods are the most economical, containing the least fat and the most preservatives. The canned foods are the most expensive (they're 75% water), usually containing the most fat and least preservatives. Semi-moist foods are expensive and high in sugar content, and I do not recommend them for any dogs.

When you're selecting a commercial diet, make sure the food

has been assessed by feeding trials for a specific life stage, not just by nutrient analysis. This statement is usually located near the ingredient label. In the United States, these trials are performed in accordance with American Association of Feed Control Officials (AAFCO), and in Canada, by the Canadian Veterinary Medical Association. This certification is important because it has been found that dog foods currently on the market that provide only a chemical analysis and calculated values but no feeding trial, may not provide adequate nutrition. The feeding trials show that the diets meet minimal, not optimal, standards; however, they are the best tests we currently have.

PUPPY REQUIREMENTS

Soon after pups are born, and certainly within the first 24 hours, they should begin nursing from their mother. This provides them with colostrum, an antibody-rich milk that helps protect them from infection for their first few months of life. Pups should be allowed to nurse for at least six weeks before they are completely weaned from their mother. Supplemental feeding may be started by as early as three weeks of age.

By two months of age, pups

should be fed puppy food. They are now in an important growth phase. Nutritional deficiencies and/or imbalances during this time of life are more devastating than at any other time. Also, this is not the time to overfeed pups or provide them with "performance" rations. Overfeeding German Shepherd Dogs can lead to serious skeletal defects such as osteochondrosis and hip dysplasia.

Pups should be fed "growth" diets until they are 12—18 months of age. Many German Shepherd Dogs do not reach adult height until 18 months of age and may continue to "fill out" until three years of age, and so, benefit from a longer period on these rations. Pups will initially need to be fed two to three meals daily until they are 12—18 months old, then once to twice daily (preferably twice) when they are converted to adult food. Proper growth diets should be selected based on acceptable feeding trials designed for growing pups. If you can't tell by reading the label, ask your veterinarian for feeding advice.

Remember that pups need "balance" in their diets. Avoid the temptation to supplement with protein, vitamins, or minerals. Calcium supplements have been implicated as a cause of bone and cartilage deformity, especially in large breed puppies. Puppy diets are already heavily fortified with calcium, and supplements tend to unbalance the mineral intake. There is more than adequate proof that these supplements are respon-

German Shepherd puppies nurse from their mother approximately 24 hours after birth and continue doing so until their teeth begin to grow in.

sible for many bone deformities seen in these growing dogs.

ADULT DIETS

The goal of feeding adult dogs is one of "maintenance." They have already done all the growing they are going to do and are unlikely to have the digestive problems of elderly dogs. In general, dogs can do well on maintenance rations containing predominantly plant- or animal-based ingredients, as long as that ration has been specifically formulated to meet maintenance level requirements. This contention should be supported by studies performed by the manufacturer in accordance with AAFCO (American Association of Feed Control Officials). In Canada, these products should be certified by the Canadian Veterinary Medical Association to meet maintenance requirements.

There's nothing wrong with feeding a cereal-based diet to dogs on maintenance rations; they are the most economical. Soy is a common ingredient in cereal-based diets but may not be completely digested by all dogs, especially German Shepherd Dogs. This causes no medical problems, although German Shepherd Dogs may tend to be more flatulent on these diets. German Shepherd Dogs may also have trouble digesting starch (associated with small intestinal bacterial overgrowth) or fat (associated with exocrine pancreatic insufficiency).

When comparing maintenance rations, it should be appreciated that these diets must meet the "minimal" require-

ments for confined dogs, not necessarily optimal levels. Most dogs will benefit when fed diets that contain easily digested ingredients that provide nutrients at least slightly above minimal requirements. Typically, these foods will be intermediate in price between the most expensive super-premium diets and the cheapest generic diets. Select only those diets that have been substantiated by feeding trials to meet maintenance requirements, those that contain wholesome ingredients, and those recommended by your veterinarian. Don't select based on price alone, on company advertising, or on total protein content.

GERIATRIC DIETS

German Shepherd Dogs are considered elderly when they are about seven years of age. There are certain changes that occur as dogs age that alter their nutritional requirements. As pets age, their metabolism slows and must be accounted for. If maintenance rations are fed in the same amounts while metabolism is slowing, weight gain may result. Obesity is the last thing one wants to contend with in an elderly pet, since it increases their risk of several other health-related problems. As pets age, most of their organs do not function as well as in youth. The digestive system, liver, pancreas, and gallbladder are not functioning at peak effect. The intestines have more difficulty extracting all the nutrients from the food consumed. A gradual decline in kidney function is considered a normal part of aging.

A responsible approach to geriatric nutrition is to realize that degenerative changes are a normal part of aging. Our goal is to minimize the potential damage done by taking this into account while the dog is still well. If we wait until an elderly dog is ill before we change the diet, we have a much harder job.

Elderly dogs need to be treated as individuals. While some benefit from the nutrition found in "senior" diets, others might do better on the highly-digestible puppy or super-premium diets. These latter diets provide an excellent blend of digestibility and amino acid content, but unfortunately, many are higher in salt and phosphorus than the older pet really needs.

Older dogs are also more prone to developing arthritis, and therefore, it is important not to overfeed them, since obesity puts added stress on the joints. For animals with joint pain, supplementing the diet with fatty acid combinations containing cis-linoleic acid, gamma-linolenic acid, and eicosapentaenoic acid can be quite beneficial.

An active German Shepherd Dog may not do well on a "maintenance" diet and may require a high-performance diet. Be sure to ask your veterinarian what the preferred feedings are for the particular activity level of your individual dog.

MEDICAL CONDITIONS AND DIET

It is important to keep in mind that dietary choices can affect the development of orthopedic diseases such as hip dysplasia, cervical vertebral instability, and osteochondrosis. When feeding a pup at risk, avoid high-calorie diets and try to feed several times a day rather than ad libitum. Sudden growth spurts are to be avoided because they result in joint instability. Recent research has also suggested that the electrolyte balance of the diet may also play a role in the development of hip dysplasia. Rations that had more balance between the positively and negatively charged elements in the diet (e.g., sodium, potassium, chloride) were less likely to promote hip dysplasia in susceptible dogs. Also, avoid supplements of calcium, phosphorus, and vitamin D as they can interfere with normal bone and cartilage development. The fact is that calcium levels in the body are carefully regulated by hormones (such as calcitonin and parathormone) as well as vitamin D. Supplementation disturbs this normal regulation and can cause many problems. It has also been shown that calcium supplementation can interfere with the proper absorption of zinc from the intestines. If you really feel the need to supplement your dog, select products such as eicosapentaenoic/gamma-linolenic fatty acid combinations or small amounts of vitamin C.

Small intestinal bacterial overgrowth is not uncommon in the German Shepherd Dog, although the cause is not completely determined. It may be associated with a relative lack of a specific antibody group (IgA) in the intestines or associated with a variety of other intestinal diseases to which they are prone, including lymphocytic-plasmacytic enteritis, eosinophilic enteritis, and exocrine pancreatic insufficiency. Preliminary studies show that by supplementing the diet with 1% fructo-oligosaccharides (FOS) and limiting the amount of cornstarch in the diet, bacterial numbers can be reduced in the intestines. Fructo-oligosaccharides are not digested by dogs, but are metabolized by intestinal bacteria. This affects the population dynamics of these microbes. Few commercial pet food companies have implemented the concept and produced diets featuring supplemental FOS and less cornstarch.

Diet can't prevent bloat (gastric dilatation/volvulus), but changing feeding habits can make a difference. Initially, the bloat occurs when the stomach becomes distended with swallowed air. This air is swallowed as a consequence of gulping food or water, stress, and exercising too close to mealtime. This is where we can make a difference. Divide meals and feed them three times daily rather than all at once. Soak dry dog food in water before feeding to decrease the tendency to gulp the food. If you want to feed dry food only, add some large clean chew toys to the feed bowl so that the dog has to "pick" to get at the food and can't gulp it. Putting the food bowl on a stepstool, so the dog doesn't have to stretch to get the food, may also be helpful. Finally, don't allow any exercise for at least one hour before and after feeding.

Zinc is an important mineral when it comes to immune function and wound healing, but it has some other uses in the German Shepherd Dog. Zinc administration, particularly zinc acetate, can also promote copper excretion from the body. Usually this is not necessary or even desirable, but some German Shepherd Dogs have an inherited disease that causes them to store copper in their livers; the result can be chronic hepatitis. Although this copper-induced hepatitis cannot be cured, zinc supplementation can be used as a safe and effective form of therapy.

Fat supplements are probably the most common supplements purchased from pet supply stores. They frequently promise to add luster, gloss, and sheen to the coat, and consequently, make dogs look healthy. The only fatty acid that is essential for this purpose is cis-linoleic acid, which is found in flaxseed oil, sunflower seed oil, and safflower oil. Corn oil is a suitable, but less effective, alternative. Most of the other oils found in retail supplements are high in saturated and monounsaturated fats and are not beneficial for shiny fur or healthy skin. For dogs with allergies, arthritis, high blood pressure (hypertension), high cholesterol, and some heart ailments, other fatty acids may be prescribed by a veterinarian. The important ingredients in these products are gamma-linolenic acid (GLA), eicosapentaenoic acid (EPA), and docosahexaenoic acid (DHA). These products have gentle and natural anti-inflammatory properties. But don't be fooled by imitations. Most retail fatty acid supplements do not contain these functional forms of the essential fatty acids—look for gamma-linolenic acid, eicosapentaenoic acid, and docosahexaenoic acid on the label.

HEALTH

**PREVENTIVE MEDICINE AND HEALTH CARE
FOR YOUR GERMAN SHEPHERD**

Keeping your German Shepherd Dog healthy requires preventive health care. This is not only the most effective, but the least expensive way to battle illness. Good preventive care starts even before puppies are born. The dam should be well cared for, vaccinated, and free of infections and parasites. Hopefully, both parents were screened for important genetic

Facing page: Your German Shepherd is dependent on you, his owner, for keeping his good health. Regular visits to your veterinarian and preventive health care will help your dog live a longer and happier life with you.

36

diseases (e.g. von Willebrands's disease), registered with the appropriate agencies (e.g., OFA, GDC, CERF), showed no evidence of medical or behavioral problems, and were found to be good candidates for breeding. This gives the pup a good start in life. If all has been planned well, the dam will pass on resistance to disease to her pups that will last for the first few months of life. However, the dam can also pass on parasites, infections, genetic diseases, and more.

TWO TO THREE WEEKS OF AGE

By two to three weeks of life, it is usually necessary to start pups on a regimen to control worms. Although dogs benefit from this parasite control, the primary reason for doing this is human health. After whelping, the dam often sheds large numbers of worms even if she tested negative previously. This is because many worms lay dormant in tissues, and the stress of delivery causes parasite release into the environment. Because studies have shown that 75% do, assume that all puppies potentially have worms. Thus, we institute worm control early to protect the people in the house from worms more than the pups themselves. The deworming is re-

peated every two to three weeks until your veterinarian feels the condition is under control. Nursing bitches should be treated at the same time because they often shed worms during this time. Only use products recommended by your veterinarian. Over-the-counter parasiticides have been responsible for deaths in pups.

SIX TO TWENTY WEEKS OF AGE

Most puppies are weaned from their mother at six to eight weeks of age. Weaning shouldn't be done too early, so that pups have the opportunity to socialize with their littermates and dam. This is important for them to be able to respond to other dogs later in life. There is no reason to rush the weaning process, unless the dam can't produce enough milk to feed the pups.

Pups are usually first examined by the veterinarian at six to eight weeks of age, which is when most vaccination schedules commence. If pups are exposed to many other dogs at this young age, veterinarians often opt for vaccinating with inactivated parvovirus at six weeks of age. When exposure isn't a factor, most veterinarians would rather wait to see the pup at eight weeks of age. At this point, they can also do a preliminary dental evaluation to see that all the puppy teeth are coming in correctly, check to see that the testicles are properly descending in males, and that there are no dict which pups are most anxious and fearful. Some form of temperament evaluation is important because behavioral problems account for more animals being euthanized (killed)

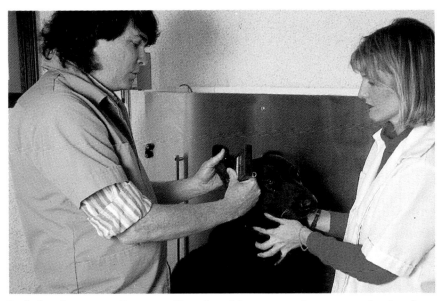

By bringing your German Shepherd to your vet on a regular basis, a good rapport is built between dog and doctor.

health reasons to prohibit vaccination at this time. Heart murmurs, wandering knee-caps (luxating patellae), juvenile cataracts, and hernias are usually evident by this time.

Your veterinarian may also be able to perform temperament testing on the pup by eight weeks of age, or recommend someone to do it for you. Although temperament testing is not completely accurate, it can often predict which pups are most anxious each year than all medical conditions combined.

Recently, some veterinary hospitals have been recommending neutering pups as early as six to eight weeks of age. A study done at the University of Florida College of Veterinary Medicine over a span of more than four years concluded there was no increase in complications when animals were neutered when less than six months of age. The evaluators also concluded that the surgery appeared to be less stressful when done in young pups.

Most vaccination schedules consist of injections being given at 6—8, 10—12, and 14—16 weeks of age. Ideally, vaccines should not be given closer than two weeks apart, and three to four weeks seems to be optimal. Each vaccine usually consists of several different viruses (e.g., parvovirus, distemper, parainfluenza, hepatitis) combined into one injection. Coronavirus can be given as a separate vaccination according to this same schedule, if pups are at risk. Some veterinarians and breeders advise another parvovirus booster at 18—20 weeks of age. A booster is given for all vaccines at one year of age and annually thereafter. For animals at increased risk of exposure, parvovirus vaccination may be given as often as four times a year. A new vaccine for canine cough (tracheobronchitis) is squirted into the nostrils. It can be given as early as six weeks of age, if pups are at risk. Leptospirosis vaccination is given in some geographic areas and likely offers protection for six to eight months. The initial series consists of three to four injections spaced two to three weeks apart,

starting as early as ten weeks of age. Rabies vaccine is given as a separate injection at three months of age, then repeated when the pup is one year old, then every one to three years depending on local risk and government regulation.

Between 8 and 14 weeks of age, use every opportunity to expose the pup to as many people and situations as possible. This is part of the critical socialization period that will determine how good a pet your dog will become. This is not the time to abandon a puppy for eight hours while you go to work. This is also not the time to punish your dog in any way, shape, or form.

This is the time to introduce your dog to neighborhood cats, birds, and other creatures. Hold off on exposure to other dogs until after the second vaccination in the series. You don't want your new friend to pick up contagious diseases from dogs it meets in its travels. By 12 weeks of age, your pup should be ready for social outings with other dogs. Do it! It's a great way for your dog to feel comfortable around members of its own species. Walk the streets and introduce your pup to everybody you meet. Your goal should be to introduce your dog to every type of person or situation it is likely to encounter in its life. Take it in cars, elevators, buses, subways, to parade grounds and beaches. You want it to habituate to all environments. Expose your pup to kids, teenagers, old people, people in wheelchairs, people on bicycles, people in uniforms. The more varied the exposure, the better the socialization.

Proper identification of your pet is also important, since this minimizes the risk of theft and increases the chances that your pet will be returned to you if it is lost. There are several different options. Microchip implantation is a relatively painless procedure involving the subcutaneous injection of an implant the size of a grain of rice. This implant does not act as a beacon if your pet is missing. However, if your pet turns up at a veterinary clinic or shelter and is checked with a scanner, the chip provides information about you that can be used to quickly reunite you with your pet. This method of identification is reasonably priced, permanent in nature, and performed at most veterinary clinics. Another option is tattooing which can be done on the inner ear or on the skin of the abdomen. Most purebreds are given a number by the associated registry (e.g., American

A tall fence is not always a foolproof means of keeping your German Shepherd in your yard. Gates may be left open or there may be an unknown opening from which your dog could escape. Always supervise your dog when outdoors.

Kennel Club, The Kennel Club, United Kennel Club, Canadian Kennel Club, etc.) that is used for identification. Alternatively, permanent numbers, such as social security numbers (telephone numbers and addresses may change during the life of your pet), can be used in the tattooing process. There are several different tattoo registries maintaining lists of dogs, their tattoo codes, and their owners. Finally, identifying collars and tags provide quick information, but can be separated from your pet if lost or stolen. They work best when combined with a permanent identification system such as microchip implantation or tattooing.

FOUR TO SIX MONTHS OF AGE

At 16 weeks of age, when your pup gets the last in its series of regular induction vaccinations, ask your veterinarian about evaluating the pup for hip dysplasia with the PennHip™ technique. This helps predict the risk of developing hip dysplasia as well as degenerative joint disease. German Shepherd Dog breeders have done an excellent job decreasing the incidence of hip dysplasia through routine screening and registration programs. Since anesthesia is typically required for the procedure, many veterinarians like to do the evaluation at the same time as neutering.

At this time, it is very worthwhile to perform a diagnostic test for von Willebrand's disease, an inherited disorder that causes uncontrolled bleeding. The German Shepherd Dog is also prone to hemophilia A, and both bleeding disorders can be assessed with a single blood sample. A simple blood test is all that is required, but it may need to be sent to a special laboratory to have the tests performed. You

will be extremely happy you had the foresight to have this done before neutering. If your dog does have a bleeding problem, it will be necessary to take special precautions during surgery.

SIX TO TWELVE MONTHS OF AGE

As a general rule, neuter your animal at about six months of age unless you fully intend to breed it. As we know, neutering can be safely done at eight weeks of age, but this is still not a common practice. Neutering not only stops the possibility of pregnancy and undesirable behaviors, but can prevent several health problems as well. It is a well-established fact that pups spayed before their first heat have a dramatically reduced incidence of mammary (breast) cancer. Likewise, neutered males significantly decrease their incidence of prostate disorders.

When your pet is six months of age, your veterinarian will want to take a blood sample to perform a heartworm test. If the test is negative and shows no evidence of heartworm infection, the pup will go on heartworm prevention therapy. Some veterinarians are even recommending preventive therapy in younger pups. This might be a once-a-day regimen, but newer therapies can be given on a once-a-month basis. As a bonus, most of these heartworm preventatives also help prevent internal parasites.

If your German Shepherd Dog has any patches of hair loss, your veterinarian will want to perform a skin scraping with a scalpel blade to see if any demodex mites are responsible. If there is a problem, don't lose hope; about 90% of demodicosis cases can be cured with supportive care only. However, it's important to diagnose it early before scarring results.

Another part of the six-month visit should be a thorough dental evaluation to make sure all the permanent teeth have correctly erupted. If they haven't, this will be the time to correct the problem. Correction should only be performed to make the animal more comfortable and promote normal chewing. The procedures should never be used to cosmetically improve the appearance of a dog used for show purposes or breeding.

After the dental evaluation, you should start implementing home dental care. In most cases, this will consist of brushing the teeth one or more times each week and perhaps using dental rinses. It is a sad fact that 85% of dogs over four years of age have periodontal disease and "doggy breath." In fact, it is so common that most people think it is "normal." Well, it is normal — as normal as bad breath would be in people if they never brushed their teeth. Brush your dog's teeth regularly with a special toothbrush and toothpaste, and you can greatly reduce the incidence of tartar buildup, bad breath, and gum disease. Provide the Puppy Bone™ from Nylabone® and a Gumabone® to puppies as early as eight to ten weeks. Nylabones® not only help in the proper development of the puppy's jaw and the emergence of adult teeth but help to keep the teeth clear...and the breath fresh. Better preventive care means that dogs live a long time, and they'll enjoy their sunset years more if they still have their teeth. Ask your veterinarian for details on home dental care.

THE FIRST SEVEN YEARS

At one year of age, your dog should be re-examined and have boosters for all vaccines. Your veterinarian will also want to do a very thorough physical examination to look for early evidence of problems. This might include taking radiographs (x-rays) of the hips and elbows to look for evidence of dysplastic changes.

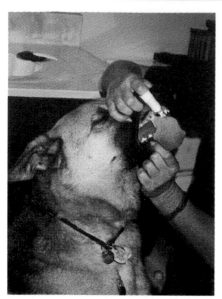

Brushing your German Shepherd's teeth will help to keep the amount of tartar build-up to a minimum. This is easy to do if your dog is cooperative.

Genetic Disease Control (GDC) will certify hips and elbows at 12 months of age; Orthopedic Foundation for Animals (OFA) won't issue certification until 24 months of age.

At 12 months of age, it's also a great time to have some blood samples analyzed to provide background information. Although few German Shepherd Dogs experience clinical problems at this young age, troubles may be starting. Therefore, it is a good idea to have baseline levels of thyroid hormones (free

and total), TSH (thyroid-stimulating hormone), blood cell counts, organ chemistries, and cholesterol levels. This can serve as a valuable comparison to samples collected in the future.

Each year, preferably around the time of your pet's birthday, it's time for a veterinary visit. This visit is a wonderful opportunity for a thorough clinical examination, rather than just "shots." Since 85% of dogs have periodontal disease by four years of age, veterinary intervention does not seem to be as widespread as it should be. The examination should include visually inspecting the ears, eyes (a great time to start scrutinizing for progressive retinal atrophy, cataracts, etc.), mouth (don't wait for gum disease), and groin; listening (auscultation) to the lungs and heart; feeling (palpating) the lymph nodes and abdomen; and answering all of your questions about optimal health care. In addition, booster vaccinations are given during these times, feces are checked for parasites, urine is analyzed, and blood samples may be collected for analysis. One of the tests run on the blood sample is for heartworm antigen. In areas of the country where heartworm is only present in the spring, summer, and fall (it's spread by mosquitoes), blood samples are collected and evaluated about a month prior to the mosquito season. Other routine blood tests are for blood cells (hematology), organ chemistries, thyroid levels, and electrolytes.

By two years of age, most veterinarians prefer to begin preventive dental cleanings, often referred to as "prophies." Anesthesia is required, and the veterinarian or veterinary dentist will use an ultrasonic scaler to remove plaque and tartar from above and below the gum line, as well as polish the teeth so that plaque has a harder time sticking to the teeth. Radiographs (x-rays) and fluoride treatments are other options. It is now known that it is plaque, not tartar, that initiates inflammation in the gums. Since scaling and root planing remove more tartar than plaque, veterinary dentists have begun using a new technique called PerioBUD (pe-riodontal bactericidal ultrasonic debridement). The ultrasonic treatment is quicker, disrupts more bacteria, and is less irritating to the gums. With tooth polishing to finish up the procedure, gum healing is better, and owners can start home care sooner. Each dog has its own dental needs that must be addressed, but most veterinary dentists recommend prophies annually. Be sure too that your German Shepherd always has a Nylabone® available to do his part in keeping his teeth clean.

SENIOR GERMAN SHEPHERD DOGS

German Shepherd Dogs are considered seniors when they reach about seven years of age. Usually veterinarians still only need to examine them once a year, but it is now important to start screening for geriatric problems. Accordingly, blood profiles, urinalysis, chest radiographs (x-rays), and electrocardiograms (EKG) are recommended on an annual basis. When problems are caught early, they are much more likely to be successfully managed. This is as true in canine medicine as it is in human medicine.

Raised dental tips on dog bones work wonders with controlling plaque in a German Shepherd. Only get the largest Plaque Attacker™ for your German Shepherd.

MEDICAL PROBLEMS

**RECOGNIZED GENETIC CONDITIONS
SPECIFICALLY RELATED TO THE GERMAN SHEPHERD**

Many conditions appear to be especially prominent in German Shepherd Dogs. Sometimes it is possible to identify the genetic basis of a problem, but in many cases, we must be satisfied with merely identifying the breeds that are at risk and how the conditions can be identified,

**Facing page:
Your puppy's
vaccination
schedule should
begin at six to
eight weeks of
age and con-
tinue until 14 to
16 weeks of age.**

treated, and prevented. Following are some conditions that have been recognized as being common in the German Shepherd Dog, but this listing is certainly not complete. Also, many genetic conditions may be common in certain breed lines, not in the breed in general.

ACRAL LICK DERMATITIS

Few things are as frustrating to veterinarians as dealing with acral lick dermatitis (lick granuloma), a problem caused by a dog licking incessantly at a spot on its leg. The dog starts licking at a spot, and before you know it, it has removed layers of skin, leaving a raw open area. The reason for this is unknown, but many theories have come and gone, and we're still not positive why a dog would do this kind of damage to itself.

German Shepherd Dogs are one of the more common breeds affected with this disorder, and males are affected twice as often as females. Some recent research has even shown that there may be some nerve deficits in dogs that develop this condition. Other research has suggested that boredom may be a precipitating cause that eventuates in a compulsive behavior.

It is important to diagnose these cases carefully, since some

cases may actually be a result of another disease condition that needs to be addressed. Often biopsies, microbial cultures, and even radiographs (x-rays) are needed to help confirm a diagnosis.

Treatment is often frustrating because it is difficult to predict the chances of success without knowing the cause. Most therapies use anti-inflammatory agents, but a variety of other options exist, including tranquilizers, female sex hormones, anti-anxiety drugs, and medications that reverse the effects of narcotics. More exotic treatments such as injecting cobra antivenin into the site, radiation therapy, and cryosurgery have been used in the past, but often have limited success. The newest craze is to use anti-anxiety drugs and antidepressants to treat the "compulsive" aspect of the disorder.

Prevention is difficult because the ultimate cause of the problem has not been determined. Until we know more, our advice must be that affected dogs, their parents, and their siblings should not be used in breeding programs.

AORTIC STENOSIS

Aortic stenosis is a congenital heart defect in which fibrous tissue impedes the flow of blood out of the heart. One of the breeds in which it is most commonly reported is the German Shepherd Dog. Genetic studies have demonstrated that at least two genes are involved, one of which is autosomal dominant (only requires one parent to be the carrier). Some affected pups may seem fairly normal, while others show all the classic symptoms of heart failure. A family history is usually evident. Veterinarians may suspect the diagnosis based on hearing the classic heart murmur, but the diagnosis can be confirmed by ultrasound examination of the heart (echocardiography) and usually by radiography (x-rays) as well. There is no standard approach to treatment. Mildly affected animals usually require no treatment at all. Others may benefit from the use of beta-blockers to help control the symptoms (but not cure the problem). More severely affected pups require heart surgery prior to six months of age before permanent changes in the heart are evident. Affected animals, their siblings, and parents should not be used in any breeding programs.

CATARACTS

Cataracts refer to an opacity or cloudiness on the lens of the eye, and ophthalmologists are careful to categorize them on the basis of stage, age of onset, and location. In German Shepherd Dogs, cataracts can be inherited as a dominant trait (with variable expressivity), meaning that only one parent need carry the trait for pups to be affected. The cataracts are usually evi-

A canine ophthalmologist can detect cataracts in German Shepherds prior to one year of age. Cataract removal surgery is available and quite successful if needed.

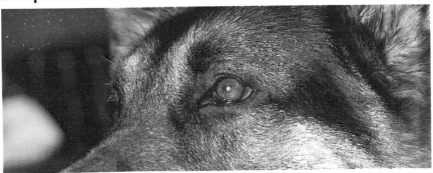

dent quite early, often in young pups, but almost always before one year of age. There is another juvenile form of cataracts in the breed, which is a recessive trait requiring both parents to be carriers. Many dogs adapt well to cataracts, but cataract removal surgery is available and quite successful if needed. Affected animals and their siblings should obviously not be used for breeding, and careful ophthalmologic evaluation of both parents is warranted.

DEMODICOSIS

Demodex mites are present on the skin of all dogs, but in some animals born with a defective immune system the numbers increase and begin to cause problems. German Shepherd Dogs are usually cited as one of the most common breeds affected with this condition. Although it is thought to be genetically transmitted, the mode of transmission has never been conclusively demonstrated.

Most cases of demodicosis are seen in young pups, and fully 90% of cases self-cure with little or no medical intervention by the time these dogs reach immunologic maturity at 18—36 months of age. In these cases, it is suspected that the immune system is marginally compro-

mised and eventually matures getting the condition under control. On the other hand, some pups (about 10% of those initially affected) do not get better and, in fact, become progressively worse. These are thought to have more severe immunologic compromise and are often labeled as having "generalized demodicosis."

The diagnosis is easily made by scraping the skin with a scalpel blade and looking at the collected debris under a microscope. The demodex mites are cigar-shaped and are easily seen. What is harder to identify is the immunologic defect that allowed the condition to occur in the first place. Recent research has suggested the problem may be linked to a decrease in interleukin-2 response, but the genetics is still a question.

If the cause of the immune dysfunction can be cured, the mange will resolve on its own. Likewise, if the pup outgrows its immunologic immaturity or defect, the condition will self-cure. This process can best be assisted by ensuring a healthy diet is being fed, treating for any internal parasites or other diseases, and perhaps using cleansing shampoos and nutritional supplements that help bolster the immune system. However, if

Since the German Shepherd Dog breed has been burdened by many potential congenital diseases, only dogs screened for these conditions should be allowed to breed.

the condition does not resolve on its own, or if it is getting worse despite conservative therapy, special mite-killing treatments are necessary. Amitraz is the most common dip used, but experimentally, milbemycin oxime and ivermectin given daily have shown some promising results. It must be remembered that killing the mites will not restore the immune system to normal.

It is best not to breed dogs with a history of demodicosis, and dogs with generalized demodicosis should *never* be bred. Although the genetic nature of this disease has not been decisively proven, it doesn't make sense to add affected individuals to the gene pool of future generations.

ELBOW DYSPLASIA

Elbow dysplasia doesn't refer to just one disease, but rather an entire complex of disorders that affect the elbow joint. Several different processes might be involved, including ununited anconeal process, fragmented medial coronoid process, osteochondritis of the medial humeral condyle, or incomplete ossification of the humeral condyle. Elbow dysplasia and osteochondrosis are disorders of young dogs, with problems usually starting between four and seven months of age. The usual manifestation is a sudden onset of lameness. In time, the continued inflammation results in arthritis in those affected joints.

German Shepherd Dogs have a particularly high incidence of elbow dysplasia. As of December 31, 1994, the Orthopedic Foundation for Animals determined that 18.2% of female German Shepherd Dogs and 23.9% of male German Shepherd Dogs assessed had evidence of elbow dysplasia on radiographs (x-rays).

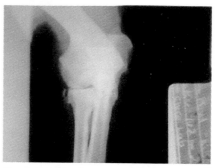

Fragmented coronoid process of the elbow, a manifestation of elbow dysplasia. Courtesy of Dr. Jack Henry.

Radiographs (x-rays) are taken of the elbow joints and submitted to a registry for evaluation. The Orthopedic Foundation for Animals (OFA) will assign a breed registry number to those animals with normal elbows that are over 24 months of age. Abnormal elbows are reported as grade I to III, where grade III elbows have well-developed degenerative joint disease (arthritis). Normal elbows on individuals 24 months or older are assigned a breed registry number and are periodically reported to parent breed clubs. Genetic Disease Control for Animals (GDC) maintains an open registry for elbow dysplasia and assigns a registry number to those individuals with normal elbows at 12 months of age or older. Only animals with "normal" elbows should be used for breeding.

There is strong evidence to support the contention that OCD (osteochondritis dissecans) of the elbow is an inherited disease likely controlled by many genes. Preliminary research (in Labrador Retrievers) also suggests that the different forms of elbow dysplasia are inherited independently. Therefore, breeding stock should be selected from those animals without a history of osteochondrosis, preferably for several generations. Unaffected dogs producing offspring with OCD, FCP (fragmented coronoid process), or both should not be bred again, and unaffected first-degree relatives (e.g., siblings) should not be used for breeding either.

Other than genetics, the most likely associations made to date suggest that feeding diets high in calories, calcium, and protein promote the development of osteochondrosis in susceptible dogs. Also, animals that are allowed to exercise in an unregulated fashion are at increased risk, since they are more likely to sustain cartilage injuries.

The management of dogs with OCD is a matter of much debate and controversy. Some recommend surgery to remove the damaged cartilage before permanent damage is done. Others recommend conservative therapy of rest and pain-killers. The most common drugs used are aspirin and polysulfated glycosaminoglycans. Most veterinarians agree that the use of cortisone-like compounds (corticosteroids) creates more problems than it treats in this condition. What seems clear is that some dogs will respond to conservative therapies, while others need surgery. Surgery is often helpful if performed before there is significant joint damage.

EPILEPSY

Idiopathic epilepsy runs in families, and breeding studies have shown a genetic basis for the disorder in German Shepherd Dogs. It is most often first seen in dogs between one and three years of age. The condition is similar to that reported in people, and the seizures follow the same pattern.

The generalized seizure usually involves certain phases. The aura is the first phase. In this phase the animal may appear restless, fearful, abnormally affectionate, or show other behavioral changes. The ictus phase, the actual seizure phase, follows the aura. Here the animal usually loses consciousness, and its limbs become stiff. This is followed by paddling movements of the limbs. Crying, urination, defecation, and salivation may also occur. This phase may last from seconds to minutes. The final phase is post-ictus. During this phase one may see confusion, circling, blindness, or sleepiness. It may last from several minutes to a few days. There is no apparent correlation between the length of the post-ictus phase and the length or severity of the ictus phase.

The diagnosis is made by pairing a history of seizures with normal test results for other potential causes. The most common anti-seizure medication used in veterinary medicine is phenobarbital. It is very good at preventing seizures and has few side effects. The animal may have an increase in appetite and thirst and, occasionally, temporary weakness while becoming accustomed to the drug. It is important to periodically check the level of phenobarbital in the blood. This is done by taking a blood sample immediately before giving the anticonvulsant medication so the concentration of drug is measured when lowest. This blood level shows whether the amount of drug given needs to be increased, decreased, or remain the same. Primidone and potassium bromide are considered options for animals that don't respond well to phenobarbital. Although complete elimination of seizure activity may not be achieved, it is still important to reduce the seizures in both intensity and frequency as much as possible. Affected animals should not be used for breeding.

EXOCRINE PANCREATIC INSUFFICIENCY

The pancreas is most recognized for its production of insulin, but it also produces important enzymes that aid in the digestion of food. In some circumstances, dogs do not make enough enzymes for their digestive needs. This is what is referred to as exocrine pancreatic insufficiency. The German Shepherd Dog is the most common breed affected, and the genetic form of the disorder is typically seen in younger dogs, usually less than two years of age.

Animals with exocrine pancreatic insufficiency (EPI) tend to eat a lot yet lose weight. They don't produce enough of the digestive enzymes to break down the nutrients in their diet to forms they can use. Also, most affected dogs have loose stools that look more like cow-pies than dog feces. The diagnostic test of choice is called the serum trypsin-like immunoreactivity (TLI) test. The condition is treated by lifelong addition of pancreatic enzymes to the diet to do the job that the pancreas has stopped doing. Special diets that are low in fiber and those formulated for dogs with small intestinal bacterial overgrowth are often the most efficiently utilized by affected dogs. No research has ever shown that low-fat diets improve the situation. Vitamin supplements that provide vitamin B_{12} (cobalamin), beta-carotene, and vitamin E may be added to the regimen at your veterinarian's discretion. Affected dogs should not be used for breeding.

GASTRIC DILATATION/ VOLVULUS

Gastric dilatation (bloat) occurs when the stomach becomes distended with air. The air gets swallowed into the stomach when susceptible dogs exercise, gulp their food/water, or are stressed. Although bloat can occur at any age, it becomes more common as susceptible dogs get older. Purebreds are three times more likely to suffer from bloat than mutts. Although German Shepherd Dogs are susceptible to the condition and frequently appear in lists of "breeds most prone to bloat," recent large surveys have found that German Shepherd Dogs are not as prone as other deep-chested breeds such as Great Danes, Weimaraners, Saint Bernards, Gordon Setters, Irish Setters, Boxers, and Standard Poodles.

Bloat on its own is uncomfortable, but it is the possible consequences that make it life-threatening. As the stomach fills with air, like a balloon, it can twist on itself and impede the flow of food within the stomach as well as the blood supply to the stomach and other digestive organs. This twisting (volvulus or torsion) not only makes the bloat worse, but also results in toxins being released into the bloodstream and death of blood-deprived tissues. These events, if allowed to progress, will usually result in death in four to six hours. Approximately one-third of dogs with bloat and volvulus will die, even under

Encourage your puppy to eat in a calm manner so as not to gulp his food and swallow air—this is a wise precaution to avoid bloat at an older age.

appropriate hospital care.

Affected dogs will be uncomfortable, restless, depressed, and have extended abdomens. They need veterinary attention immediately, or they will suffer from shock and die! There are a variety of surgical procedures to correct the abnormal positioning of the stomach and organs. Intensive medical therapy is also necessary to treat for shock, acidosis, and the effects of toxins.

Bloat can't be completely prevented, but there are some easy things to do to greatly reduce the risk. Don't leave food down for dogs to eat as they wish. Divide the day's meals into three portions and feed morning, afternoon, and evening. Try not to let your dog gulp its food; if necessary, add some chew toys to the bowl so he has to work around them to get the food. Add water to dry food before feeding. Have fresh clean water available all day but not at mealtime. Do not allow exercise for one hour before and after meals. Following this feeding advice may actually save your dog's life. In addition to this information, there have been no studies that support the contention that soy in the diet increases the risk of bloat. Soy is relatively poorly digested and can lead to flatulence, but the gas accumulation in bloat comes from swallowed air, not gas produced in the intestines.

HEMOPHILIA

Hemophilia is a bleeding disorder associated with a lack of a specific clotting factor (factor VIII). It is a sex-linked disease in which females pass on the defect to their sons. The condition is relatively rare, but German Shepherd Dogs are one of the breeds in which the disorder is most commonly reported. A screening test is available to detect affected animals as well as carriers. There are no cures for hemophilia, and management can be intensive as well as expensive. Affected animals should not be used for breeding and neither should the mother. Other family members should be screened for carrier status prior to being considered for breeding.

HIP DYSPLASIA

Hip dysplasia is a genetically transmitted developmental problem of the hip joint that is common in many breeds. Dogs may be born with a "susceptibility" or "tendency" to develop hip dysplasia, but it is not a foregone conclusion that all susceptible dogs will eventually develop hip dysplasia. All dysplastic dogs are born with normal hips, and the dysplastic changes begin within the first 24 months of life, although they are usually evident long before then.

It is now known that there are several factors that help determine whether a susceptible dog will ever develop hip dysplasia. These include body size, conformation, growth patterns, caloric load, and electrolyte balance in the dog food.

Based on research tabulated up to January, 1995, the Orthopedic Foundation for Animals concluded that 20.8% of the radiographs submitted from German Shepherd Dogs had evidence of hip dysplasia. Although this is an improvement from the situation 20 years ago, there is still a lot of room for improvement.

When purchasing a German Shepherd Dog pup, it is best to ensure that the parents are both registered with normal hips through one of the international registries such as the Orthopedic Foundation for Animals or Genetic Disease Control. Pups over 16 weeks of age can be tested by veterinarians trained in the PennHip™ procedure, which is a way of predicting risk of developing hip dysplasia and arthritis.

If you start with a pup with less risk of hip dysplasia, you can further reduce your risk by controlling its environment. Select a food with a moderate amount of protein, and avoid the super high premium and high-calorie diets. Also, feed your pup several times a day for defined periods (e.g., 15 minutes) rather than leaving the food down all day. Avoid all nutritional supplements, especially those that include calcium, phosphorus, and/or vitamin D. Use controlled exercise for your pup rather than letting him run loose. Unrestricted exercise can stress the pup's joints, which are still developing.

If you have a dog with hip dysplasia, all is not lost. There is much variability in the clinical presentation. Some dogs with severe dysplasia experience little pain, while others that have minor changes may be extremely sore. The main problem is that dysplastic hips promote degenerative joint disease (osteoarthritis or osteoarthrosis), which can eventually incapacitate the joint. Aspirin and other anti-inflammatory agents are suitable in the early stages. Surgery is needed when animals are in great pain, when drug therapy doesn't work adequately, or when movement is severely compromised.

HYPERTROPHIC CARDIOMYOPATHY

Hypertrophic cardiomyopathy is a heart disease in which the septum of the left ventricle becomes thickened and obstructs the flow of blood within the heart chamber. German Shepherd Dogs are the most common breed affected. Whereas dilated cardiomyopathy is more common and seen in a variety of breeds, this form is rarer and has more similarity to the disease seen in cats. The end result is eventual heart failure. The diagnosis can usually be confirmed with ultrasound examinations of the heart (echocardiography). Beta-blockers give some symptomatic relief, but there is currently no cure for the condition, in people or dogs. The roles of L-carnitine, taurine, and coenzyme Q_{10} have not been demonstrated for cases of hypertrophic cardiomyopathy. Affected animals should not be used for breeding.

HYPERTROPHIC OSTEODYSTROPHY

Hypertrophic osteodystrophy is a disease of young, primarily large-breed dogs. German Shepherd Dogs appear to be the most common breed affected. They are typically affected at a young age, often at three to four months of age. The condition is associated with inflammation of affected bones and a derangement of normal bone development.

The cause of hypertrophic osteodystrophy is the subject of much debate. It is thought that an infectious process is most likely, but no organisms have been consistently isolated. Other theories suggest that it may be involved with a relative imbalance of vitamin C, or result from excessive supplementation with other vitamins and minerals. Yet others suggest that it is a genetically conditioned defect of bone growth.

Affected dogs experience lameness, often in the wrist areas (distal radius and ulna) of the front legs. The upper leg bones may be swollen, warm, and painful. Affected dogs may experience anorexia, fever, depression, and even simple weight loss. These signs may come and go in an intermittent pattern. The diagnosis is confirmed by radiography (x-rays). Blood panels may have increased serum alkaline phosphatase levels, but calcium and phosphorus levels are usually normal. This helps differentiate this condition from panosteitis.

Because the cause of this condition is not known, there are no specific treatments. Episodes often last a week, and complete, spontaneous remissions have been reported. Affected dogs are placed on a balanced diet and often treated with anti-inflammatory agents (e.g., aspirin) and cage rest.

HYPOTHYROIDISM

Hypothyroidism is the most commonly diagnosed endocrine (hormonal) problem in the German Shepherd Dog. The disease itself refers to an insufficient amount of thyroid hormones being produced. Although there are several different potential causes, lymphocytic thyroiditis is by far the most common. Iodine deficiency and goiter are extremely rare. In lymphocytic thyroiditis, the body produces antibodies that target aspects of thyroid tissue. The process usually starts between one and three years of age in affected animals but doesn't become clinically evident until later in life.

There is a great deal of misinformation about hypothyroidism. Owners often expect their dogs to be obese and otherwise don't suspect the condition. The fact is that hypothyroidism is quite variable in its manifestations, and obesity is only seen in a small percentage of cases. In most cases, affected animals appear fine until they use up most of their remaining thyroid hormone reserves. The most common manifestations, then, are lack of energy and recurrent infections. Hair loss is seen in about one-third of cases.

You might suspect that hypothyroidism would be easy to diagnose, but it is trickier than you think. Since there is a large reserve of thyroid hormones in the body, a test measuring only total blood levels of the hormones (T-4 and T-3) is not a very sensitive indicator of the condition. Thyroid stimulation tests are the best way to measure the functional reserve. Measuring "free" and "total" levels of the hormones or TSH (thyroid-stimulating hormone) are other approaches. Also, since we know that most cases are due to antibodies produced in the body, screening for these autoantibodies can help identify animals at risk of developing hypothyroidism.

Because this breed is so prone to developing hypothyroidism, periodic screening for the disorder is warranted in many cases. Although none of the screening tests are perfect, a basic panel evaluating total T-4, free T-4, TSH, and cholesterol levels is a good start. Ideally, this would first be performed at one year of

You will know when your German Shepherd Dog is not feeling well. Any deviation from his normal actions or habits should be taken as a warning and your veterinarian should be contacted.

age and annually thereafter. This screening is practical because none of these tests are very expensive.

Fortunately, although there may be some problems in diagnosing hypothyroidism, treatment is straightforward and relatively inexpensive. Supplementing the affected animal twice daily with thyroid hormones effectively treats the condition. In many breeds, supplementation with thyroid hormones is commonly done to help confirm the diagnosis. Animals with

hypothyroidism should not be used in a breeding program, and those with circulating autoantibodies, but no actual hypothyroid disease, should also not be used for breeding.

IGA DEFICIENCY

Selective deficiency of immunoglobulin A (IgA), a class of antibody, can result in respiratory, skin, or digestive tract disease. The German Shepherd Dog is one of the breeds most commonly reported with this condition. The low circulating levels of antibody predispose affected individuals to developing a variety of infections. It is thought that IgA deficiency may also be linked to the high incidence of small intestinal bacterial overgrowth (SIBO) seen in the breed.

In all likelihood, IgA deficiency is more common than most breeders and veterinarians expect because they aren't routinely testing for it. As more and more laboratories offer valid and reasonably-priced tests for IgA levels, awareness should grow. However, since this is such an important disorder and so easily diagnosed, prospective pet owners should ask for evaluation of IgA levels in a pre-purchase (or post-purchase) examination. Starting out in life with a healthy immune system is one of the most important qualities of any animal. There are no specific treatments for the condition. Since the genetics of the condition are not fully known, affected animals and their immediate family should not be used in breeding programs.

LIVER DISEASE

Some dogs are prone to developing liver disease in association with an inherited metabolic defect, which causes copper to accumulate in the liver and lead to toxicity. This is similar to Wilson's disease in people. The German Shepherd Dog is not the breed affected most often (that would be the Bedlington Terrier), but the incidence is high enough to warrant mention here. The condition is spread as a recessive trait, therefore, both parents must be carriers if a dog is found to be affected.

Affected dogs develop a slowly-progressive form of liver disease. They are usually in young adulthood when the condition is first recognized. Jaundice only develops late in the course of the disease when liver function is severely compromised.

Very recently, researchers have discovered a genetic marker for copper toxicosis that can be detected by a blood test. Although not yet widely available as a commercial test, this laboratory evaluation is an exceptionally important method for detecting carriers of the dis-

From head to paws your German Shepherd should be checked over by you at least once a week. Interdigital cysts, excessively long nails, or foreign objects imbedded can all affect your Shepherd's feet.

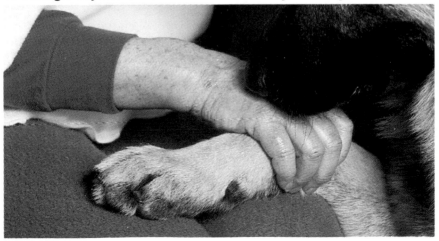

ease. Those carriers should be removed from all breeding possibilities, at which time it should be possible to completely eliminate the trait in German Shepherd Dogs.

NODULAR DERMATOFIBROSIS

Nodular dermatofibrosis is a condition most commonly seen in German Shepherd Dogs and has been recognized since 1967. This condition evolves as a series of lumps most often seen involving the areas between the toes and on the legs. The lumps are usually painless but can become ulcerated. Although the lumps don't cause many problems themselves, they are typically associated with the development of malignant cancers of the kidney and/or uterus.

Any German Shepherd Dog having lumps on its legs should be evaluated for the possibility of nodular dermatofibrosis. No dogs with this condition should be used for breeding, and all should be screened for the present or future development of kidney or uterine tumors. Affected animals should be evaluated at least every three months, since with early recognition, the kidney tumors may be surgically removed before the cancer has had time to spread.

PANNUS

Pannus, also known as chronic superficial keratitis, refers to a condition in which pigment and blood vessels grow across the cornea appearing like a dark film. The most common breed affected with pannus is the German Shepherd Dog. The cause of the condition is still a matter of much debate. It is believed that genetics may play some role, but studies have not shown the condition to be passed from generation to generation. The role of ultraviolet light and immune reactivity also are being considered. A recent European study found virus-like particles in the eyes of affected dogs, but actual viruses could not be recovered.

In most cases, the condition involves dark pigment infiltrating the clear cornea, usually starting at the outer edge and moving inward. In time, blood vessels grow into the cornea where none existed previously. The end result is a dark scarring eye disease which, fortunately, is not usually too painful. Diagnosis is not difficult, but consultation with a veterinary ophthalmologist may be warranted when considering treatment options. Some owners have even had opticians customize UV-protecting clear polycarbonate sunglasses for their pets. Affected dogs should not be used for breeding, even though genetic studies have not proven that the condition is heritable.

PANOSTEITIS

Panosteitis is an inflammatory condition that affects the but occasionally they may be as old as six years of age when first affected. They typically show lameness that may affect one or more legs and may appear to "migrate" between legs. Pain is severe in some dogs, mild in others. Associated problems are

The German Shepherd Dog is particularly prone to panosteitis. Although signs of lameness typically occur before one year, a German Shepherd may be affected as late as six years of age.

leg bones. The German Shepherd Dog is the most common breed affected. The condition affects males more frequently than females and is often recurrent or periodic in nature. Most dogs are less than a year of age, lack of appetite, weight loss, and muscle wasting. The diagnosis can usually be confirmed by radiography (x-rays).

There is no specific treatment for panosteitis, but the condition usually responds to enforced rest and mild anti-inflammatory agents (e.g., aspirin). Many breeders recommend the use of diets with lower protein and fat contents, but a dietary role for the condition has not been established. Affected dogs should not be used for breeding.

PATENT DUCTUS ARTERIOSUS

Patent ductus arteriosus (PDA) is the most common congenital heart defect in the dog and is the result of the activities of several different genes. It results when the normal fetal communication between the non-functional lungs and the aorta fails to close after birth. This causes blood to be shunted into the pulmonary artery which effectively floods the lungs with blood, while the rest of the body receives less than needed. Most pups don't have too many symptoms, and the diagnosis is made during the first veterinary visit in which a classic type of heart murmur is evident. Electrocardiograms (EKG), radiographs (x-rays), and ultrasound examinations (echocardiography) can all be used to confirm a diagnosis. The problem can be surgically corrected, and there is a 90% success rate with appropriate heart surgery. Affected dogs should not be used for breeding.

SMALL INTESTINAL BACTERIAL OVERGROWTH

Small intestinal bacterial overgrowth (SIBO) is emerging as an important cause of chronic diarrhea in the dog, and the German Shepherd Dog is the breed affected most often. The reasons for this are unclear. It is known that German Shepherds are prone to a variety of other intestinal ills as well as IgA deficiency. It is currently hypothesized that the combination may be the trigger for the development of SIBO. However, this is just a hypothesis, and the whole story is far from complete. Other assertions suggest links to achlorhydria (lack of stomach acid), excessive antibiotic therapy, stagnant loop syndrome, and exocrine pancreatic insufficiency.

Regardless of initiating cause, the proliferation of bacteria in the small intestine affects the absorption of nutrients from this region of bowel. Affected dogs may have difficulty digesting starch, fats may be broken down to hydroxy fatty acids, and bile salts may be deconjugated. All can result in diarrhea. The diagnosis is not straightforward. One of the first screening tests run is blood levels of the vitamins folate and cobalamin. Typically, serum levels of folate are elevated while those of cobalamin are depressed. Confirmation may require quantitative bacterial culture of intestinal fluids; biopsies used don't reveal changes that can confirm the diagnosis. Researchers are looking at a hydrogen breath test for dogs similar to the one used in people. Initial results are encouraging.

Medication can be given orally either as a liquid or in pill or capsule form.

Treatment for SIBO involves antibiotic administration (e.g., tetracycline) and feeding a diet low in carbohydrates (sugars and starches) and fats. Good quality protein sources and rice usually make up the basis of a therapeutic diet. Fructo-oligosaccharides (FOS) are natural compounds found in various plants and make an excellent alternative to starch, when used in diets for dogs with SIBO. Eventual relapse likely means that the underlying condition was never addressed. Affected dogs should not be used for breeding.

VON WILLEBRAND'S DISEASE

The most commonly inherited bleeding disorder of dogs is von Willebrand's disease (vWD). The abnormal gene can be inherited from one or both parents. If both parents pass on the gene, most of the resultant pups fail to thrive and will die. In most cases, however, the pup inherits a relative lack of clotting ability, which is quite variable. For instance, one dog may have 15% of the clotting factor, while another might have 60%. The higher the amount, the less likely it will be that the bleeding will be readily evident, since spontaneous bleeding is usually only seen when dogs have less than 30% of the normal level of von Willebrand clotting factor. Thus, some dogs don't get diagnosed until they are neutered or spayed, and they end up bleeding uncontrollably or they develop pockets of blood (hematomas) at the surgical site.

There are tests available to determine the amount of von Willebrand factor in the blood that are accurate and reasonably priced. German Shepherd Dogs used for breeding should have normal amounts of von Willebrand factor in their blood. Carriers should not be used for breeding, even if they appear clinically normal. Since hypothyroidism can be linked with von Willebrand's disease, thyroid profiles can also be a useful part of the screening procedure in older German Shepherds.

OTHER CONDITIONS SEEN IN THE GERMAN SHEPHERD

- Aspergillus terreus infection
- Cauda equina syndrome
- Chemodectoma
- Chondrosarcoma
- Cleft lip/palate
- Colitis
- Coloboma
- Congenital vestibular disease
- Corneal dystrophy
- Cutaneous asthenia
- Cystinuria
- Degenerative myelopathy
- Dermoid
- Diabetes mellitus
- Ectropion
- Esophageal motility disorders
- Euryblepharon
- Eversion of third eyelid cartilage
- Familial vasculopathy
- Furunculosis/cellulitis
- Giant axonal neuropathy
- Glycogen storage disease
- Hemangiosarcoma
- Hemophilia B
- Intersex
- Intervertebral disk disease
- Lens luxation
- Lupoid onychodystrophy
- Lupus erythematosus (cutaneous/discoid)
- Malassezia dermatitis
- Mandibular distoclusion (overbite)
- Oligodontia
- Optic nerve hypoplasia
- Osteosarcoma
- Pedal panniculitis
- Pemphigus erythematosus
- Perianal fistulae
- Persistent right aortic arch
- Pituitary dwarfism
- Progressive retinal atrophy (generalized)
- Progressive retinal atrophy (central)
- Retinal dysplasia (retinal folds)
- Sebaceous adenitis
- Seborrhea
- Seminoma
- Silica urolithiasis
- Third eyelid conjunctivitis
- Tumoral calcinosis (calcinosis circumscripta)
- Vaginal edema/prolapse

Facing page: Since many diseases known to the German Shepherd are inherited, it is important that you purchase your pup from sound breeding stock that has been fully certified against the congenital diseases.

INFECTIONS & INFESTATIONS

**HOW TO PROTECT YOUR GERMAN SHEPHERD
FROM PARASITES AND MICROBES**

An important part of keeping your German Shepherd Dog healthy is to prevent problems caused by parasites and microbes. Although there are a variety of drugs available that can help limit problems, prevention is always the desired option. Taking the proper precautions leads to

Facing page: Good grooming will keep your German Shepherd's coat looking its best and keep you abreast of his skin condition.

less aggravation, less itching, and less expense.

FLEAS

Fleas are important and common parasites but not an inevitable part of every pet-owner's reality. If you take the time to understand some of the basics of flea population dynamics, control is both conceivable and practical.

Fleas have four life stages (egg, larva, pupa, adult), and each stage responds to some therapies while being resistant to others. Failing to understand this is the major reason why some

people have so much trouble getting the upper hand in the battle to control fleas.

Fleas spend all their time on the host animal (in this case, your dog) and only leave if physically removed by brushing, bathing, or scratching. However, the eggs that are laid on the animal are not sticky and fall to the ground to contaminate the environment. Our goal must be to remove fleas from the animals in the house, from the house itself, and from the immediate outdoor environment. Part of our plan must also involve using different medications to get rid

Fleas are commonly found in grass. Give your pet a thorough going over before he comes back into your home.

of the different life stages, as well as minimizing the use of potentially harmful insecticides that could be poisonous for pets and family members.

A flea comb is a very handy device for recovering fleas from pets. The best places to comb are the tailhead, groin area, armpits, back, and neck region. Fleas collected should be dropped into a container of alcohol which quickly kills them before they can escape. In addition, all pets should be bathed with a cleansing shampoo (or flea shampoo) to remove fleas and eggs. This, however, has no residual effect, and fleas can jump back on immediately after the bath if nothing else is done. Rather than using potent insecticidal dips and sprays, consider products containing the safe pyrethrins, imidacloprid or fipronil and the insect growth regulators (such as methoprene and pyripoxyfen or insect development inhibitors (IDIs) such as lufenuron. These products are not only extremely safe, but the combination is effective against eggs, larvae, and adults. This only leaves the pupal stage to cause continued problems. Insect growth regulators can also be safely given as once-a-month oral preparations. Electronic flea collars are not to be recommended for any dogs.

Vacuuming is a good first step to cleaning up the household because it picks up about 50% of the flea eggs and it also stimulates flea pupae to emerge as adults, a stage when they are easier to kill with insecticides. The vacuum bag should then be removed and discarded with each treatment. Household treatment can then be initiated with pyrethrins and a combination of either insect growth regulators or sodium polyborate (a borax derivative). The pyrethrins need to be reapplied every two to three weeks, but the insect growth regulators last about two to three months, and many companies guarantee sodium polyborate for a full year. Stronger insecticides, such as carbamates and organophosphates, can be used and will last three to four weeks in the household, but they are potentially toxic and offer no real advantages other than their persistence in the home environment (this is also one of their major disadvantages).

When an insecticide is combined with an insect growth regulator, flea control is most likely to be successful. The insecticide kills the adult fleas, and the insect growth regulator affects the eggs and larvae. However, insecticides kill less than 20% of

Your flea problem means that not only the dog needs to be treated but the dog's bedding, your carpeting and furniture as well.

flea cocoons (pupae). Because of this, new fleas may hatch in two to three weeks despite appropriate application of products. This is known as the "pupal window," and is one of the most common causes for ineffective flea control. This is why a safe insecticide should be applied to the home environment two to three weeks after the initial treatment. This catches the newly hatched pupae before they have a chance to lay eggs and perpetuate the flea problem.

If treatment of the outdoor environment is needed, there are several options. Pyripoxyfen an insect growth regulator, is stable in sunlight and can be used outdoors. Sodium polyborate can be used as well, but it is important that it not be inadvertently eaten by pets. Organophosphates and carbamates are sometimes recommended for outdoor use, and it is not necessary to treat the entire property. Flea control should be directed predominantly at garden margins, porches, dog houses, garages, and other pet lounging areas. Fleas don't do well with direct exposure to sunlight so generalized lawn treatment is not needed. Finally, microscopic worms (nematodes) are available that can be sprayed onto the lawn with a garden sprayer. The nematodes eat immature flea forms and then biodegrade without harming anything else.

TICKS

Ticks are found world wide and can cause a variety of problems including blood loss, tick paralysis, Lyme disease, "tick fever," Rocky Mountain spotted fever, and babesiosis. All are important diseases that need to be prevented whenever possible. This is only possible by limiting the exposure of our pets to ticks.

For those species of tick that dwell indoors, the eggs are laid mostly in cracks and on vertical surfaces in kennels and homes. Most other species are found outside in vegetation, such as grassy meadows, woods, brush, and weeds.

Ticks feed only on blood, but they don't actually bite. They attach to an animal by sticking their harpoon-shaped mouth parts into the animal's skin, and then they suck blood. Some ticks can increase their size 20—50 times as they feed. Favorite places for them to locate are between the toes and in the ears, although they can appear anywhere on the skin surface.

A good approach to prevent ticks is to remove underbrush and leaf litter, and to thin the trees in areas where dogs are allowed. This removes the cover and food sources for small mammals that serve as hosts for ticks. Ticks must have adequate cover that provides high levels of moisture and at the same time provides an opportunity of contact with animals. Keeping the lawn

well maintained also makes ticks less likely to drop by and stay.

Because of the potential for ticks to transmit a variety of harmful diseases, dogs should

Outdoor areas with an abundance of trees and brush can be highly infested with ticks. Be sure to inspect your German Shepherd after inhabiting such areas.

be carefully inspected after walks through wooded areas (where ticks may be found), and careful removal of all ticks is very important in the prevention of disease. Care should be taken not to squeeze, crush, or puncture the body of the tick, since exposure to body fluids of ticks may lead to spread of any disease carried by that tick to the animal or to the person removing the tick. The tick should be disposed of in a container of alcohol or flushed down the toilet. If the site becomes infected, veterinary attention should be sought immediately. Insecticides and repellents should only be applied to pets following appropriate veterinary advice, since indiscriminate use can be dangerous. Recently, a new tick collar has become available that contains amitraz. This collar not only kills ticks, but causes them to retract from the skin within two to three days. This greatly reduces the chances of ticks transmitting a variety of diseases. A spray formulation has also recently been developed and marketed. It might seem that there should be vaccines for all the diseases carried by ticks, but only a Lyme disease (*Borrelia burgdorferi)* formulation is currently available.

MANGE

Mange refers to any skin condition caused by mites. The contagious mites include ear mites, scabies mites, cheyletiella mites, and chiggers. Demodectic mange is associated with proliferation of demodex mites, but they are not considered contagious. Demodicosis is covered in more detail in the chapter on breed-related medical conditions.

The most common causes of mange in dogs are ear mites, which are extremely contagious. The best way to avoid ear mites is to buy pups from sources that don't have a problem with ear mite infestation. Otherwise, pups readily acquire them when kept in crowded environments in which other animals might be carriers. Treatment is effective if whole body (or systemic) therapy is used, but relapses are common when medication in the ear canal is the only approach. This is because the mites tend to crawl out of the ear canal when medications are instilled. They simply feed elsewhere on the body until it is safe for them to return to the ears.

Scabies mites and cheyletiella mites are passed on by other dogs that are carrying the mites. They are "social" diseases that can be prevented by avioding exposure of your dog to others that are infested. Scabies (sarcoptic mange) has the dubious honor of being the most itchy disease to which dogs are susceptible. Chigger mites are present in forested areas, and dogs acquire them by roaming in these areas. All can be effectively diagnosed and treated by your veterinarian should your dog happen to become infested.

HEARTWORM

Heartworm disease is caused by the worm *Dirofilaria immitis* and is spread by mosquitoes. The female heartworms produce microfilariae (baby worms) that circulate in the bloodstream, waiting to be picked up by mosquitoes to pass the infection along. Dogs do not get heartworm by socializing with infected dogs; they only get infected by mosquitoes that carry the infective microfilariae. The adult heartworms grow in the heart and major blood vessels and eventually cause heart failure.

Fortunately, heartworm is easily prevented by safe oral medications that can be administered daily or on a once-a-month basis. The once-a-month preparations also help prevent many of the common intestinal parasites, such as hookworms, roundworms, and whipworms.

Prior to giving any preventative medication for heartworm, an antigen test (an immunologic test that detects heartworms) should be performed by a veterinarian, since it is dangerous to give the medication to dogs that harbor the parasite. Some experts also recommend a microfilarial test just to be doubly certain. Once the test results show that the dog is free of heartworms, the preventative therapy can be commenced. The length of time the heartworm preventatives must be given depends on the length of the mosquito season. In some parts of the country, dogs are on preventative therapy year round. Heartworm vaccines may soon be available, but the preventatives now available are easy to administer, inexpensive, and quite safe.

INTESTINAL PARASITES

The most important internal parasites in dogs are roundworms, hookworms, tapeworms, and whipworms. Roundworms are the most common. It has been estimated that 13 trillion roundworm eggs are discharged in dog feces every day! Studies have shown that 75% of all pups carry roundworms and start shedding them by three weeks of age. People are infected by exposure to dog feces containing infective roundworm eggs, not by handling pups. Hookworms can cause a disorder known as cutaneous larva migrans in people. In dogs, they are most dangerous to puppies, since they latch onto the intestines and suck blood. They can cause anemia and even death when they are present in large numbers. The most common tapeworm is *Dipylidium caninum*, which is spread by fleas. However, another tapeworm *(Echinococcus multilocularis)* can cause fatal disease in people and can be spread to people from dogs. Whipworms live in the lower aspects of the intestines. Dogs get whipworms by consuming infective larvae. However, it may be another three months before they start shedding them in their stool, greatly complicating diagnosis. In other words, dogs can be infected by whipworms, but fecal evaluations are usually negative until the dog starts passing those eggs three months after being infected.

Other parasites, such as coccidia, cryptosporidium, giardia, and flukes can also cause problems in dogs. The best way to prevent all internal parasite problems is to have pups dewormed according to your veterinarian's recommendations and parasite checks done on a regular basis, at least annually.

VIRAL INFECTIONS

Dogs get viral infections such as distemper, hepatitis, parvovirus, and rabies by exposure to infected animals. The key to prevention is controlled exposure to other animals and, of course, vaccination. Today's vaccines are extremely effective,

and properly vaccinated dogs are at minimal risk for contracting these diseases. However, it is still important to limit exposure to other animals that might be harboring infection. When selecting a facility for boarding or grooming an animal, make sure they limit their clientele to animals that have documented vaccine histories. This is in everyone's best interest. Similarly, make sure your veterinarian has a quarantine area for infected dogs and that animals aren't admitted for surgery, boarding, grooming, or diagnostic testing without up-to-date vaccinations. By controlling exposure and ensuring vaccination, your pet should be safe from these potentially devastating diseases.

It is beyond the scope of this book to settle all the controversies of vaccination, but they are worth mentioning. Should vaccines be combined in a single injection? It's convenient and cheaper to do it this way, but might some vaccine ingredients interfere with others? Some say yes, some say no. Are vaccine schedules designed for convenience or effectiveness? Mostly convenience. Some ingredients may only need to be given every two or more years, research is incomplete. Should the dose of the vaccine vary with weight, or should a Chihuahua receive the same dose as a German Shepherd Dog? Good questions, no definitive answers. Finally, should we be using modified-live or inactivated vaccine products? There is no short answer for this debate. Ask your veterinarian, and do a lot of reading yourself!

CANINE COUGH

Canine infectious tracheobronchitis, also known as canine cough and kennel cough, is a contagious viral/bacterial disease that results in a hacking cough that may persist for many weeks. It is common wherever dogs are kept in close quarters, such as kennels, grooming parlors, dog shows, training classes, and even veterinary clinics. The condition doesn't respond well to most medications, but eventually clears spontaneously over the course of many weeks. Pneumonia is a possible but uncommon complication.

Prevention is best achieved by limiting exposure and utilizing vaccination. The fewer opportunities you give your dog to come in contact with others, the less the likelihood of getting infected. Vaccination is not foolproof because many different viruses can be involved. Parainfluenza virus is included in most vaccines and is one of the more common viruses known to initiate the condition. *Bordetella bronchiseptica* is the bacterium most often associated with tracheobronchitis, and a vaccine is now available that needs to be repeated twice yearly for dogs at risk. This vaccine is squirted into the nostrils to help stop the infection before it gets deeper into the respiratory tract. Make sure the vaccination is given several days (preferably two weeks) before exposure to ensure maximum protection.

Your German Shepherd Dog will be a member of your family for many years. It is important that he be treated with respect and cared for as any other member of the family would be.

FIRST AID by Judy Iby, RVT

**KNOWING YOUR DOG IN GOOD HEALTH
& BEING PREPARED FOR EMERGENCIES**

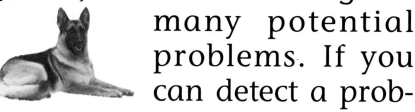

With some experience, you will learn how to give your dog a physical at home, and consequently will learn to recognize many potential problems. If you can detect a problem early, you can seek timely medical help and thereby decrease your dog's risk of developing a more serious problem.

Facing page: Regular visits to the veterinarian ensure that your German Shepherd Dog remains in the best possible condition. Your German Shepherd Dog depends on you for his continued good health.

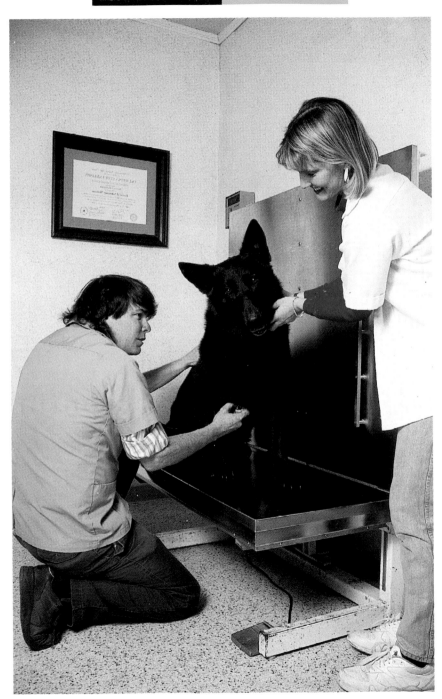

Every pet owner should be able to take his pet's temperature, pulse, respirations, and check the capillary refill time (CRT). Knowing what is normal will alert the pet owner to what is abnormal, and this can be life saving for the sick pet.

TEMPERATURE

The dog's normal temperature is 100.5 to 102.5 degrees Fahrenheit. Take the temperature rectally for at least one minute. Be sure to shake the thermometer down first, and you may find it helpful to lubricate the end. It is easy to take the temperature with the dog in a standing position. Be sure to hold on to the thermometer so that it isn't expelled or sucked in. A dog could have an elevated temperature if he is excited or if he is overheated; however, a high temperature could indicate a medical emergency. On the other hand, if the temperature is below 100 degrees, this could also indicate an emergency.

CAPILLARY REFILL TIME AND GUM COLOR

It is important to know how your dog's gums look when he is healthy, so you will be able to recognize a difference if he is not feeling well. There are a few breeds, among them the Chow

Your German Shepherd's temperature is taken rectally for at least one minute. A normal temperature is 100.5—102.5°F.

Chow and its relatives, that have black gums and a black tongue. This is normal for them. In general, a healthy dog will have bright pink gums. Pale gums are an indication of shock or anemia and are an emergency. Likewise, any yellowish tint is an indication of a sick dog. To check capillary refill time (CRT) press your thumb against the dog's gum. The gum will blanch out (turn white) but should refill (return to the normal pink color) in one to two seconds. CRT is very important. If the refill time is slow and your dog is acting poorly, you should call your veterinarian immediately.

HEART RATE, PULSE, AND RESPIRATIONS

Heart rate depends on the breed of the dog and his health. Normal heart rates range from about 50 beats per minute in the larger breeds to 130 beats per minute in the smaller breeds. You can take the heart rate by pressing your fingertips on the dog's chest. Count for either 10 or 15 seconds, and then multiply by either 6 or 4 to obtain the rate per minute. A normal pulse is the same as the heart rate and is taken at the femoral artery located on the insides of both rear legs. Respirations should be observed and depending on the size and breed of the dog should be 10 to 30 per minute. Obviously, illness or excitement could account for abnormal rates.

PREPARING FOR AN EMERGENCY

It is a good idea to prepare for an emergency by making a list and keeping it by the phone. This list should include:

1. Your veterinarian's name, address, phone number, and office hours.
2. Your veterinarian's policy for after-hour care. Does he take his own emergencies or does he refer them to an emergency clinic?
3. The name, address, phone number and hours of the emergency clinic your veterinarian uses.

Your German Shepherd's normal heart rate will increase during exercise or play. If a resting dog's breathing or heart rate seems abnormal, contact your veterinarian immediately.

4. The number of the National Poison Control Center for Animals in Illinois: 1-800-548-2423. It is open 24 hours a day.

In a true emergency, time is of the essence. Some signs of an emergency may be:

1. Pale gums or an abnormal heart rate.
2. Abnormal temperature, lower than 100 degrees or over 104 degrees.
3. Shock or lethargy.
4. Spinal paralysis.

A dog hit by car needs to be checked out and probably should have radiographs of the chest and abdomen to rule out pneumothorax or ruptured bladder.

EMERGENCY MUZZLE

An injured, frightened dog may not even recognize his owner and may be inclined to bite. If your dog should be injured, you may need to muzzle him to protect yourself before you try to handle him. It is a good idea to practice muzzling the calm, healthy dog so you understand the technique. Slip a lead over his head for control. You can tie his mouth shut with something like a two-foot-long bandage or piece of cloth. A necktie, stocking, leash or even a piece of rope will also work.

1. Make a large loop by tying a loose knot in the middle of the bandage or cloth.
2. Hold the ends up, one in each hand.
3. Slip the loop over the dog's muzzle and lower jaw, just behind his nose.
4. Quickly tighten the loop so he can't open his mouth.
5. Tie the ends under his lower jaw.
6. Make a knot there and pull the ends back on each side of his face, under the ears, to the back of his head.

If he should start to vomit, you will need to remove the muzzle immediately. Otherwise, he could aspirate vomitus into his lungs.

ANTIFREEZE POISONING

Antifreeze in the driveway is a potential killer. Because antifreeze is sweet, dogs will lap it up. The active ingredient in antifreeze is ethylene glycol, which causes irreversible kidney damage. If you witness your pet ingesting antifreeze, you should call your veterinarian immediately. He may recommend that you induce vomiting at once by using hydrogen peroxide, or he may recommend a test to confirm antifreeze ingestion. Treatment is aggressive and must be administered promptly if the dog is to live, but you wouldn't want to subject your dog to unnecessary treatment.

BEE STINGS

A severe reaction to a bee sting (anaphylaxis) can result in difficulty breathing, collapse and even death. A symptom of a bee sting is swelling around the muzzle and face. Bee stings are antihistamine responsive. Over-the-counter antihistamines are available. Ask your veterinarian for recommendations on safe anthistamines to use and doses to administer. You should monitor the dog's gum color and respirations and watch for a decrease in swelling. If your dog is showing signs of anaphylaxis, your veterinarian may need to give him an injection of corticosteroids. It would be wise to call your veterinarian and confirm treatment.

BLEEDING

Bleeding can occur in many forms, such as a ripped dewclaw, a toenail cut too short, a puncture wound, a severe laceration, etc. If a pressure bandage is needed, it must be released every 15–20 minutes. Be careful of elastic bandages since it is easy to apply them too tightly. Any bandage material should be clean. If no regular

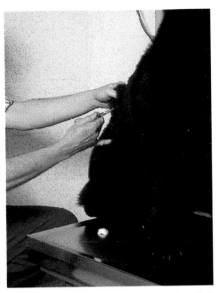

Your German Shepherd should be taken to the veterinarian annually for its vaccinations and a general physical.

bandage is available, a small towel or wash cloth can be used to cover the wound and bind it with a necktie, scarf, or something similar. Styptic powder, or even a soft cake of soap, can be used to stop a bleeding toenail. A ripped dewclaw or toenail may need to be cut back by the veterinarian and possibly treated with antibiotics. Depending on their severity, lacerations and puncture wounds may also need professional treatment. Your first thought should be to clean the wound with peroxide, soap and water, or some other antiseptic cleanser. Don't use alcohol.

BLOAT

Although not generally considered a first aid situation, bloat can occur in a dog rather suddenly. Truly, it is an emergency! Gastric dilatation-volvulus or gastric torsion—the twisting of the stomach to cut off both entry and exit, causing the organ to "bloat," is a disorder primarily found in the larger, more deep-chested breeds. It is life threatening and requires immediate veterinary assistance.

BURNS

If your dog gets a chemical burn, call your veterinarian immediately. Rinse any other burns with cold water and if the burn is significant, call your veterinarian. It may be necessary to clip the hair around the burn so it will be easier to keep clean.

You can cleanse the wound on a daily basis with saline and apply a topical antimicrobial ointment, such as silver sulfadiazine 1 percent cream or gentamicin cream. Burns can be debilitating, especially to an older pet. They can cause pain and shock. It takes about three weeks for the skin to slough after the burn and there is the possibility of permanent hair loss.

CARDIOPULMONARY RESUSCITATION (CPR)

Check to see if your dog has a heart beat, pulse and spontaneous respiration. If his pupils are already dilated and fixed, the prognosis is less favorable. This is an emergency situation that requires two people to administer lifesaving techniques. One person needs to breathe for the

Puppies need rest. Don't overtax your new puppy and allow him enough recuperation time after play periods.

A German Shepherd that is not feeling well may mope about and not act like himself. His crate will be a welcome haven for recovery.

dog while the other person tries to establish heart rhythm. Mouth to mouth resuscitation starts with two initial breaths, one to one and a half seconds in duration. After the initial breaths, breathe for the dog once after

Make the ailing dog as comfortable as possible. A speedy recovery is just around the corner.

every five chest compressions. (You do not want to expand the dog's lungs while his chest is being compressed.) You inhale, cover the dog's nose with your mouth, and exhale *gently*. You should see the dog's chest expand. Sometimes, pulling the tongue forward stimulates respiration. You should be ventilat-

ing the dog 12–20 times per minute. The person managing the chest compressions should have the dog lying on his right side with one hand on either side of the dog's chest, directed over the heart between the fourth and fifth ribs (usually this is the point of the flexed elbow). The number of compressions administered depends on the size of the patient. Attempt 80–120 compressions per minute. Check for spontaneous respiration and/or heart beat. If present, monitor the patient and discontinue resuscitation. If you haven't already done so, call your veterinarian at once and make arrangements to take your pet in for professional treatment.

CHOCOLATE TOXICOSIS

Dogs like chocolate, but chocolate kills dogs. Its two basic chemicals, caffeine and theobromine, overstimulate the dog's nervous system. Ten ounces of milk chocolate can kill a 12-pound dog. Symptoms of poisoning include restlessness, vomiting, increased heart rate, seizure, and coma. Death is possible. If your dog has ingested chocolate, you can give syrup of ipecac at a dosage of one-eighth of a teaspoon per pound to induce vomiting. Two tablespoons of hydrogen peroxide is an alternative treatment.

CHOKING

You need to open the dog's mouth to see if any object is visible. Try to hold him upside down to see if the object can be dislodged. While you are working on your dog, call your veterinarian, as time may be critical.

need to be seen by the veterinarian, and some may require antibiotics. It is important that you learn if the offending dog has had a rabies vaccination. This is important for your dog, but also for you, in case you are the victim. Wash the wound and call your doctor for further instructions. You should check on your tetanus vaccination history.

Be aware of what your child is eating while your German Shepherd is about. Chocolate is toxic to dogs—never give them even a taste!

DOG BITES

If your dog is bitten, wash the area and determine the severity of the situation. Some bites may need immediate attention, for instance, if it is bleeding profusely or if a lung is punctured. Other bites may be only superficial scrapes. Most dog bite cases

Rarely, and I mean rarely, do dogs get tetanus. If the offending dog is a stray, try to confine him for observation. He will need to be confined for ten days. A dog that has bitten a human and is not current on his rabies vaccination cannot receive a rabies vaccination for ten days.

Dog bites should be reported to the Board of Health.

DROWNING

Remove any debris from the dog's mouth and swing the dog, holding him upside

Electrical cords may be a source of electrocution. This photo shows a cord too close to the crate. A dog could pull it in and begin to chew on it.

down. Stimulate respiration by pulling his tongue forward. Administer CPR if necessary, and call your veterinarian. Don't give up working on the dog. Be sure to wrap him in blankets if he is cold or in shock.

ELECTROCUTION

You may want to look into puppy proofing your house by installing GFCIs (Ground Fault Circuit Interrupters) on your electrical outlets. A GFCI just saved my dog's life. He had pulled an extension cord into his crate and was "teething" on it at seven years of age. The GFCI kept him from being electrocuted. Turn off the current before touching the dog. Resuscitate him by administering CPR and pulling his tongue forward to stimulate respiration. Try mouth-to-mouth breathing if the dog is not breathing. Take him to your veterinarian as soon as possible since electrocution can cause internal problems, such as lung damage, which need medical treatment.

EYES

Red eyes indicate inflammation, and any redness to the upper white part of the eye (sclera) may constitute an emergency. Squinting, cloudiness to the cornea, or loss of vision could indicate severe problems, such as glaucoma, anterior uveitis and episcleritis. Glaucoma is an emergency if you want to save the dog's eye. A prolapsed third eyelid is abnormal and is a symptom of an underlying problem. If something should get in your dog's eye, flush it out with cold water or a saline eye wash. Epiphora and allergic conjunctivitis are annoying and frequently persistent problems. Epiphora (excessive tearing) leaves the area below the eye wet and sometimes stained. The wetness may lead to a bacterial infection. There are numerous causes (allergies, infections, foreign matter, abnormally located eyelashes and adjacent facial hair that rubs against the eyeball, defects or diseases of the tear drainage system, birth defects of the eyelids, etc.) and the treatment is based on the cause. Keeping the hair around the eye cut short and sponging the eye daily will give relief. Many cases are responsive to medical treat-

ment. Allergic conjunctivitis may be a seasonal problem if the dog has inhalant allergies (e.g., ragweed), or it may be a year 'round problem. The conjunctiva becomes red and swollen and is prone to a bacterial infection associated with mucus accumulation or pus in the eye. Again keeping the hair around the eyes short will give relief. Mild corticosteroid drops or ointment will also give relief. The underlying problem should be investigated.

FISH HOOKS

An imbedded fish hook will probably need to be removed by the veterinarian. More than likely, sedation will be required along with antibiotics. Don't try to remove it yourself. The shank

Your German Shepherd Dog can cut himself on sharp objects or step on a fish hook—always be prepared for any unexpected mishaps.

of the hook will need to be cut off in order to push the other end through.

FOREIGN OBJECTS

I can't tell you how many chicken bones my first dog ingested. Fortunately she had a "cast iron stomach" and never suffered the consequences. However, she was always going to the veterinarian for treatment. Not all dogs are so lucky. It is unbelievable what some dogs will take a liking to. I have assisted in surgeries in which all kinds of foreign objects were removed from the stomach and/or intestinal tract. Those objects included socks, pantyhose, stockings, clothing, diapers, sanitary products, plastic, toys, and, last but not least, rawhides. Surgery is costly and not always successful, especially if it is performed too late. If you see or suspect your dog has ingested a foreign object, contact your veterinarian immediately. He may tell you to induce vomiting or he may have you bring your dog to the clinic immediately. Don't induce vomiting without the veterinarian's permission, since the object may cause more damage on the way back up than it would if you allow it to pass through.

HEATSTROKE

Heatstroke is an emergency! The classic signs are rapid, shallow breathing; rapid heartbeat; a temperature above 104 degrees; and subsequent collapse. The dog needs to be cooled as quickly as possible and treated immediately by the veterinarian. If possible, spray him down with cool water and pack ice around his head, neck, and groin. Monitor his temperature and stop the cooling process as soon as his temperature reaches 103 degrees. Nevertheless, you will need to keep monitoring his temperature to be sure it doesn't elevate again. If the temperature continues to drop to below 100 degrees, it could be life threatening. Get professional help immediately. Prevention is more successful than treatment. Those at the greatest risk are brachycephalic (short nosed) breeds, obese dogs, and those that suffer from cardiovascular disease. Dogs are not able to cool off by sweating as people can. Their only way is through panting and radiation of heat from the skin surface. When stressed and exposed to high environmental temperature, high humidity, and poor ventilation, a dog can suffer heatstroke very quickly. Many people do not realize how quickly a car can overheat. Never leave a dog unattended in a car. It is even against the law in some states. Also, a brachycephalic, obese, or infirm dog should never be left unattended outside during inclement weather and should have his activities curtailed. Any dog left outside, by law, must be assured adequate shelter (including shade) and fresh water.

POISONS

Try to locate the source of the poison (the container which lists the ingredients) and call your veterinarian immediately. Be prepared to give the age and weight of your dog, the quantity of poison consumed and the probable time of ingestion. Your veterinarian will want you to read off the ingredients. If you can't reach him, you can call a local poison center or the National Poison Control Center for Animals in Illinois, which is open 24 hours a day. Their phone number is 1-800-548-2423. There is a charge for their service, so you may need to have a credit card number available.

Symptoms of poisoning include muscle trembling and weakness, increased salivation, vomiting and loss of bowel control. There are numerous household toxins (over 500,000). A dog can be poisoned by toxins in

When taking your German Shepherd Dog on outings, be sure to provide protection from the sun and have plenty of fresh water available for him to drink.

the garbage. Other poisons include pesticides, pain relievers, prescription drugs, plants, chocolate, and cleansers. Since I own small dogs I don't have to worry about my dogs jumping up to the kitchen counters, but when I owned a large breed she would clean the counter, eating all the prescription medications.

Your pet can be poisoned by means other than directly ingesting the toxin. Ingesting a rodent that has ingested a rodenticide is one example. It is possible for a dog to have a reaction to the pesticides used by exterminators. If this is suspected you should contact the exterminator about the potential dangers of the pesticides used and their side effects.

Don't give human drugs to your dog unless your veterinarian has given his approval. Some human medications can be deadly to dogs.

This list was published in the American Kennel Club *Gazette*, February, 1995. As the list states these are common poisonous plants, but this list may not be complete. If your dog ingests a poisonous plant, try to identify it and call your veterinarian. Some plants cause more harm than others.

PORCUPINE QUILLS

Removal of quills is best left up to your veterinarian since it can be quite painful. Your unhappy dog would probably appreciate being sedated for the removal of the quills.

POISONOUS PLANTS

Amaryllis (bulb)	Jasmine (berries)
Andromeda	Jerusalem Cherry
Elephant Ear	Jimson Weed
English Ivy	Laburnum
Apple Seeds (cyanide)	Larkspur
Elderberry	Laurel
Arrowgrass	Locoweed
Avocado	Marigold
Azalea	Marijuana
Bittersweet	Mistletoe (berries)
Boxwood	Monkshood
Buttercup	Mushrooms
Caladium	Narcissus (bulb)
Castor Bean	Nightshade
Cherry Pits	Oleander
Chokecherry	Peach
Climbing Lily	Philodendron
Crown of Thorns	Poison Ivy
Daffodil (bulb)	Privet
Daphne	Rhododendron
Delphinium	Rhubarb
Dieffenbachia	Snow on
Dumb Cane	the Mountain
Foxglove	Stinging Nettle
Hemlock	Toadstool
Holly	Tobacco
Hyacinth (bulb)	Tulip (bulb)
Hydrangea	Walnut
Iris (bulb)	Wisteria
Japanese Yew	Yew

SEIZURE (CONVULSION OR FIT)

Many breeds, including mixed breeds, are predisposed to seizures, although a seizure may be secondary to an underlying medical condition. Usually a seizure is not considered an emergency unless it lasts longer than ten minutes. Nevertheless, you should notify your veterinarian. Dogs do not swallow their tongues. Do not handle the dog's mouth since your dog probably cannot control his actions and may inadvertently bite you. The seizure can be mild; for instance, a dog can have a seizure standing up. More frequently the

Naptime! German Shepherds may be unpredictable about where and when they want to nap. This lady has outgrown her bed or has stolen the cat's sleeping place.

dog will lose consciousness and may urinate and/or defecate. The best thing you can do for your dog is to put him in a safe place or to block off the stairs or areas where he can fall.

SEVERE TRAUMA

See that the dog's head and neck are extended so if the dog is unconscious or in shock, he is able to breathe. If there is any vomitus, you should try to get the head extended down with the body elevated to prevent vomitus from being aspirated. Alert your veterinarian that you are on your way.

SHOCK

Shock is a life threatening condition and requires immediate veterinary care. It can occur after an injury or even after severe fright. Other causes of shock are hemorrhage, fluid loss, sepsis, toxins, adrenal insufficiency, cardiac failure, and anaphylaxis. The symptoms are a rapid weak pulse, shallow breathing, dilated pupils, subnormal temperature, and muscle weakness. The capillary refill time (CRT) is slow, taking longer than two seconds for normal gum color to return. Keep the dog warm while transporting him to the veterinary clinic. Time is critical for survival.

SKUNKS

Skunk spraying is not necessarily an emergency, although it would be in my house. If the dog's eyes are sprayed, you need to rinse them well with water. One remedy for deskunking the dog is to wash him in tomato juice and follow with a soap and water bath. The newest remedy is bathing the dog in a mixture of one quart of three percent hydrogen peroxide, quarter cup baking soda, and one teaspoon liquid soap. Rinse well. There

The great outdoors can be dangerous to your German Shepherd in many ways. Wild animals, overexposure to weather conditions, and poisonous plants are just a few of the things to look out for.

are also commercial products available.

SNAKE BITES

It is always a good idea to know what poisonous snakes reside in your area. Rattlesnakes, water moccasins, copperheads, and coral snakes are residents of some areas of the United States. Pack ice around the area that is bitten and call your veterinarian immediately to alert him that you are on your way. Try to identify the snake or at least be able to describe it (for the use of antivenin). It is possible that he may send you to another clinic that has the proper antivenin.

TOAD POISONING

Bufo toads are quite deadly. You should find out if these nasty little critters are native to your area.

VACCINATION REACTION

Once in a while, a dog may suffer an anaphylactic reaction to a vaccine. Symptoms include swelling around the muzzle, extending to the eyes. Your veterinarian may ask you to return to his office to determine the severity of the reaction. It is possible that your dog may need to stay at the hospital for a few hours during future vaccinations.

RECOMMENDED READING

DR. ACKERMAN'S DOG BOOKS FROM T.F.H.

OWNER'S GUIDE TO DOG HEALTH
TS-214, 432 pages
Over 300 color photographs

Winner of the 1995 Dog Writers Association of America's Best Health Book, this comprehensive title gives accurate, up-to-date information on all the major disorders and conditions found in dogs. Completely illustrated to help owners visualize signs of illness, different states of infection, procedures and treatment, it covers nutrition, skin disorders, disorders of the major body systems (reproductive, digestive, respiratory), eye problems, vaccines and vaccinations, dental health and more.

SKIN & COAT CARE FOR YOUR DOG
TS-249, 224 pages
Over 200 color photographs

Dr. Ackerman, a specialist in the field of dermatology and a Diplomate of the American College of Veterinary Dermatology, joins 14 of the world's most respected dermatologists and other experts to produce an extremely helpful manual on the dog's skin. Coat and skin problems are extremely common in the dog, and owners need to better understand the conditions that affect their dogs' coats. The book details everything from the basics of parasites and mange to grooming techniques, medications, hair loss and more.

DOG BEHAVIOR AND TRAINING
Veterinary Advice for Owners
TS-252, 292 pages
Over 200 color photographs

Joined by co-editors Gary Landsberg, DVM and Wayne Hunthausen, DVM, Dr. Ackerman and about 20 experts in behavioral studies and training set forth a practical guide to the common problems owners experience with their dogs. Since behavioral disorders are the number-one reason for owners to abandon a dog, it is essential for owners to understand how the dog thinks and how to correct him if he misbehaves. The book covers socialization, selection, rewards and punishment, puppy-problem prevention, excitable and disobedient behaviors, sexual behaviors, aggression, children, stress and more.

RECOMMENDED READING

OTHER BOOKS FROM T.F.H.

THE BOOK OF THE GERMAN SHEPHERD DOG
by Anna Katherine Nicholas
H-1062, 300 pages
Color & b/w photographs

Anna Katherine Nicholas is one of America's most famous dog show judges and has a long-time association with the German Shepherd. In *The Book of the German Shepherd Dog* she offers impressive and detailed information about the Shepherd history, kennels world-wide, judging, showing, health care, and much more. The book remains valuable for its impressive collection of historical photographs and the information about the dogs in them.

THE GERMAN SHEPHERD DOG
by Earnest H. Hart
PS-810, 256 pages
Color & b/w photographs

Eminently readable, this book is permeated with the wit and professionalism of a dedicated author of vast experience. If you own a German Shepherd or contemplate purchasing one for show, obedience, or Schutzhund work— or just as a guard, friend and companion—*The German Shepherd Dog* is for you, for the book and the breed are inseparable.

TRAINING YOUR DOG FOR SPORTS AND OTHER ACTIVITIES
by Charlotte Schwartz
TS-258, 160 pages
Over 200 full-color photographs

In this colorful and vividly illustrated book, author Charlotte Schwartz, a professional dog trainer for 40 years, demonstrates how your pet dog can assume a useful and meaningful role in everyday life. No matter what lifestyle you lead or what kind of dog you share your life with, there's a suitable and eye-opening activity in this book for you and your dog.